Dr. Holger Reibold

eGroupWare 1.0 kompakt –

The official administrator and users guide

cover design: bomots verlag
cover photograph: Corbis
ISBN: 2-915925-08-9

Contents

Preface

With eGroupWare the Open source community has once more created a system which doesn't have to hide behind commercial solutions. On the contrary, the free groupware environment provides everything one needs for the use in the enterprise: mail functions, calendar, appointment scheduler and task management, project management functions and so on. The administrator can scoop from a pool of about thirty modules.

The efficiency of eGroupWare is proven by best ratings at reader polls of the popular Linux magazines. In May, the SourceForge project has awarded eGroupWare the title of the project of the month.

Nevertheless, until now documentation were lacking how to administrate and configure eGroupWare and how to use the different modules in practise. The onhand handbook closes this gap. It describes everything that is required for a succesful start.

The only remaining thing is to wish you much fun.

Yours,

Holger Reibold

1. Getting started

eGroupWare is a multiuser groupware environment, intended to change information inside business or organizations. Most probably it is the best business solution that is available for Linux and Windows. As one learns from Sourceforge (sourceforge.net), the eGroupWare project belongs to the most active projects. In addition, it was chosen the project of the month in May 2004. Also different Linux magazines have honored the system in the past.

eGroupWare contains a collection of applications with which one can communicate in the enterprise with other employees, to arrange, plan and manage appointments. The system is created openly and permits integrating further applications. It has an open architecture, it's an open source software, and everybody can or may edit the source code. Moreover, the software can be functionally enhanced with the help of API.

eGroupWare has arisen from a splitting-off of the phpGroupWare project in the year 2003. As a PHP based system the groupware solution sets on web and Linux standards. To access it, one needs merely a Web browser. For the most part, it obtains the data from a SQL database, mostly MySQL. In addition, eGroupWare supports PostgreSQL and MS SQL servers, soon it will also support MaxDB. In addition, a Web server is needed. Under Linux, as a rule, the Apache web server is used.

eGroupWare contains the following basic applications:

- email
- calender
- adressbook
- bookmarks
- forum
- notices
- tasks
- project management
- helpdesk/ticket system

Altogether, there are more than 30 applications avalaible.

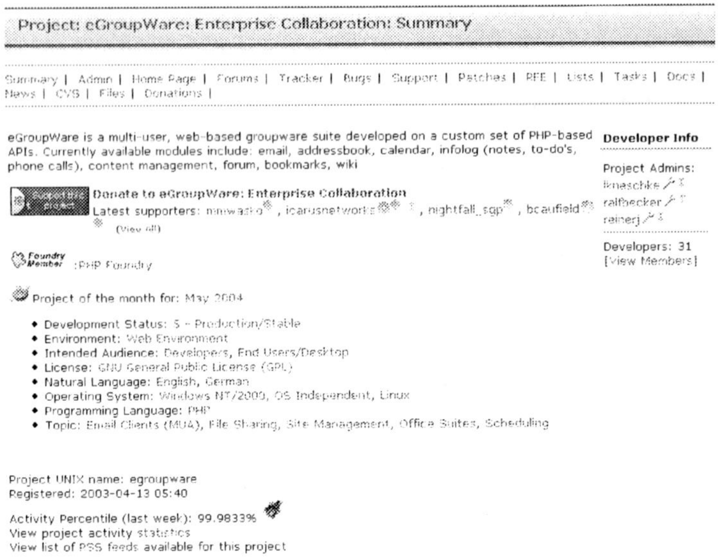

According to SourceForge (sourceforge.net/projects/egroupware/) there are more than 30 developers working on the project.

1.1 Requirements

Let us now turn to the installation and configuration of eGroupWare. Before installing eGroupWare, different requirements have to be met. At first the system needs a web server. Then you need a database. If the mail functions shall be used, a SMTP and a POP3/IMAP4 server is required. In addition, eGroupWare needs a PHP 4.2 installation. eGroupWare can be installed under Linux and also under Windows. In both cases it would be best to use a XAMPP installation. This will provide all the components that are required for running eGroupWare.

Setting up an apache server is not as easy as many people think. It's more difficult, if additional packets are needed, such as MySQL, PHP or Perl. This problem can be solved by using XAMPP. XAMPP is a particular distribution that combines Apache, MySQL, PHP and Perl und provides easy installation and implementation of these programs. XAMPP is available at the ApacheFriends website (*www.apachefriends.org*). They provide distributions for Linux, Solaris and also for Windows.

The Linux distribution has been tested under SuSE, RedHat, Mandrake and Debian and contains among others, the following programs and modules: Apache, MySQL, PHP & PEAR, Perl, ProFTPD, phpMyAdmin, OpenSSL, GD, Freetype2, libjpeg, libpng, gdbm, zlib, expat, Sablotron, libxml, Ming, Webalizer, pdf class, ncurses, mod_perl, FreeTDS, gettext, OpenLDAP (client), mcrypt, mhash, Turck MMCache, SQLite and IMAP C-Client.

1.2 Installing XAMPP

Implementing XAMPP is quite simple. We confine ourselves here to the installation under Linux. The installation under Windows is also quite simple. You will find corresponding information at the Apachefriends web site. First of all download and unpack the 23 MB package.

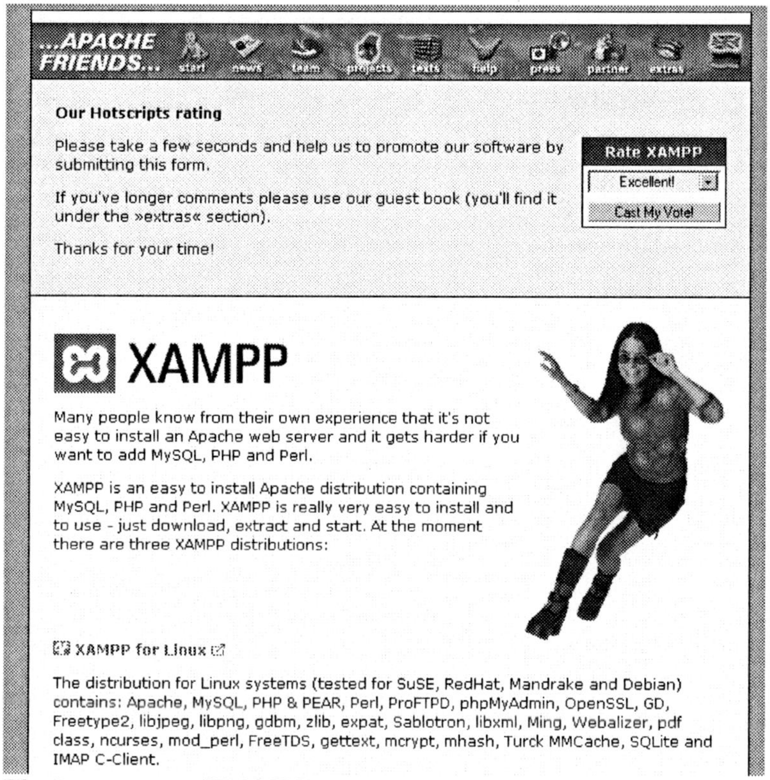

The home page of XAMPP.

In addition, an upgrade and a development package are available on the XAMPP web site. The development package contains all files one needs to translate programs for XAMPP. Moreover, the necessary manual pages are contained.

After the download merely two steps are required. First go to a Linux shell and login as the system administrator root:

```
su
```

Now the downloaded package will be unpacked and installed:

```
tar xvfz xampp-linux-1.4.4.tar.gz -C /opt
```

It is important that you do not unpack the package on a Windows computer with corresponding tools because this won't work according to the information from the Apachefriends. A XAMPP version is already installed and overwritten by the above step. The developers recommend the use of a XAMPP upgrade, though. With the two steps XAMPP is installed in the directory */opt/lampp*.

Starting XAMPP is as easy, too. You only enter the following command on the console:

```
/opt/lampp/lampp start
```

You should now see the following (or similar) messages on the screen:

```
Starting XAMPP 1.4.4...
XAMPP: Starting Apache with SSL...
XAMPP: Starting MySQL...
XAMPP: Starting ProFTPD...
XAMPP started.
```

The system is ready for use, i.e. Apache, MySQL and eventually ProFTPD are running on the system. Should there occur contrary to your expectations or problems which e.g. would be noticeable by error messages, you should take a look into the FAQ.

Next you will have to test the environment. This is very easy, too. You only start the browser and request the following URL:

```
http://localhost
```

If the system had been assigned a fixed IP adresse, *localhost* has to be replaced by this address. After this the XAMPP start page will be opened. Here you can choose between English, German and French language version. If you later replace this start page by another, the XAMPP start page will still be available at *http://localhost/xampp/* or *http://IP-Adresse/xampp/*.

The XAMPP start page welcomes the user. At the start page you will find several links to check the status of the installation, to run a security check, to start several example programs and also to access additional programs like phpMyAdmin.

Under *Demos* you will find several example programs, e.g. a CD manager, which even can convert the entries into a PDF document. Another neat program is Instant Art, a PHP GD program. Under usage of FreeType and a TrueType font, it creates nice calligraphical effects after a letter and/or a string has been entered.

If the ProFTPD FTP server has been started too, you can now access the htdocs directory of the XAMPP server with a FTP client and publish additional applications and documents on the server. The default user for this is *nobody* with the password *lampp*.

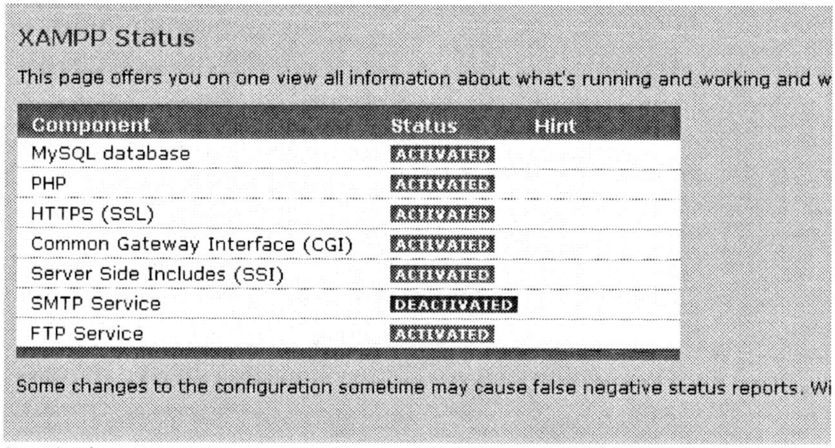

Retrieving the system status.

Originally, XAMPP has not been designed for productivity purposes, but to provide the developer a development environment which is quickly accessable and easy to manage. As a result of this, XAMPP intentionally does not pursue a restrictive security policy, but in contrary, is very openly preconfigured. This is ideal for a developer, because the system does not prescribe him rules. Especially the following XAMPP settings are intentionally set unsecure:

1. The MySQL administrator (root) does not own a password.
2. The MySQL daemon is accessable via the network.
3. The ProFTPD daemon uses the password *lampp*.
4. PhpMyAdmin is also accessable via the network.
5. MySQL and Apache run under the same user identity (nobdoy)

The actual security status of an XAMPP installation can always be retrieved via the link *security check*. Critical settings are displayed by the status *not secure* and a red marking. Secure components are displayed green. There is another colour indication: Yellow indicates that the security status could not be checked.

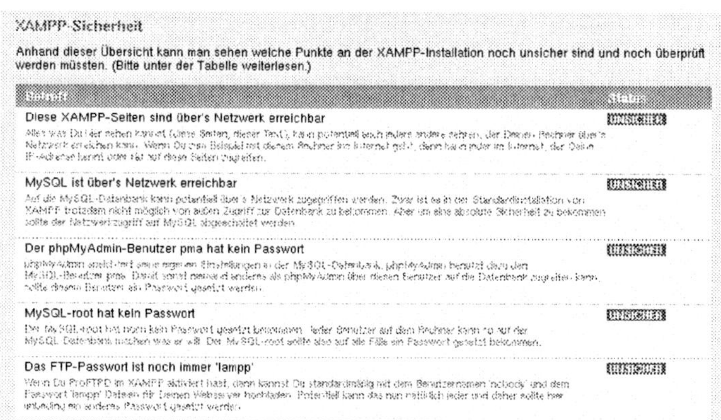

The security check of the XAMPP installation.

To adjust the security preferences especially for a deployment in a network, you should adjust the standard configuration. To do so, perform the following command:

```
/opt/lampp/lampp security
```

The command calls the dialogue driven security configuration to close all critical gaps. Here an example for a typical session:

```
linux:~ # /opt/lampp/lampp security
XAMPP: Quick security check...
XAMPP: Your XAMPP pages are NOT secured by a password.
XAMPP: Do you want to set a password? [yes] yes
XAMPP: Password:
XAMPP: Password (again):
XAMPP: Password protection active. Please use 'lampp'
as user name!
XAMPP: MySQL is accessable via network.
XAMPP: Normaly that's not recommended. Do you want me
to turn it off? [yes] yes
XAMPP: Turned off.
XAMPP: Stopping MySQL...
XAMPP: Starting MySQL...
XAMPP: The MySQL/phpMyAdmin user pma has no password
set!!!
XAMPP: Do you want to set a password? [yes] yes
XAMPP: Password:
XAMPP: Password (again):
XAMPP: Setting new MySQL pma password.
XAMPP: Setting phpMyAdmin's pma password to the new
one.
XAMPP: MySQL has no root passwort set!!!
XAMPP: Do you want to set a password? [yes] yes
XAMPP: Write the password somewhere down to make sure
you won't forget it!!!
XAMPP: Password:
XAMPP: Password (again):
XAMPP: Setting new MySQL root password.
XAMPP: Setting phpMyAdmin's root password to the new
one.
XAMPP: The FTP password is still set to 'lampp'.
XAMPP: Do you want to change the password? [yes] yes
XAMPP: Password:
XAMPP: Password (again):
XAMPP: Reload ProFTPD...
XAMPP: Done.
```

After the security settings have been adjusted, it would be good to perform a new security check. Only this way you can be sure that the changes made achieve the desired result.

XAMPP supports several start and stop parameters. They can be used with the command */opt/lampp/lampp*. The following table summarizes the parameters:

parameter	description
start	Starts XAMPP.
stop	Stops XAMPP.
restart	Stops und starts XAMPP.
reload	Apache, MySQL and – if started – ProFTPD reread their configuration file.
security	Performes a security check of the XAMPP installation and closes eventual holes.
startapache	Starts only Apache web server.
startssl	Starts Apache web server with SSL support. It will then be available at *https://localhost*. By this command SSL support will be permanently activated. Restarting XAMPP also restarts SSL.
startmysql	Starts only the MySQL database.
startftp	Starts only the ProFTPD server. The FTP server is preconfigured to upload e.g. HTML files on the XAMPP server, as user *nobody* with password *lampp*. Using this command, the FTP server will be permanently activated. Restarting XAMPP will also restart the FTP server.
stopapache	Stops Apache.
stopssl	Stops the SSL support for Apache. Restarting XAMPP also won't restart the SSL support.
stopmysql	Stops the MySQL database.
stopftp	Stops the ProFTPD server. When restarting XAMPP, the FTP server won't be restarted.
reloadapache	This command causes the Apache to reread its config file.
reloadmysql	MySQL rereads its config file.
reloadftp	This command causes the ProFTPD to reread it`s config file.

How does one use these parameters in practise? Let's have a look at an example. If you want to start the Apache with SSL support, you use this command:

```
/opt/lampp/lampp startssl
```

Afterwards the Apache is available under *https://localhost*.
Let's have a look at another example. To stop XAMPP, you only enter the following command:

```
/opt/lampp/lampp stop
```

XAMPP now displays the following (or similar) messages on the console:

```
Stopping XAMPP for Linux 1.4.4...
XAMPP: Stopping Apache...
XAMPP: Stopping MySQL...
XAMPP: Stopping ProFTPD...
XAMPP stopped.
```

Let's have a look at the different config files that can be used to customize XAMPP components. The following overview summarizes the directories and the function of the config files of the software packages contained in XAMPP. They easily allow additional customizations of the environment:

file/directory	description
/opt/lampp/bin/	XAMPP commands like e.g. */opt/lampp/bin/mysql*, which calls the MySQL monitor.
/opt/lampp/htdocs/	Documentroot directory of the Apache web server, in which the web pages are placed.
/opt/lampp/etc/httpd.conf	Apache configuration file
/opt/lampp/etc/my.cnf	MySQL configuration file
/opt/lampp/etc/php.ini	PHP configuration file
/opt/lampp/etc/proftpd.conf	ProFTPD configuration file
/opt/lampp/phpmyadmin/config.inc.php	phpMyAdmin configuration file

1.3 Installing eGroupWare

Having installed and configured XAMPP, the requirements for a succesful implementing of eGroupWare are met. Let's now turn to the setup of the groupware solution. As for the installation, the following steps are necessary:

1. First of all download the eGroupWare package. There are several packages availabe at the eGroupWare home page, along the packed archives there are also the RPM variants.
2. To install the RPM package, perform the following command: *rpm –ivh eGroupWare-x.x.x-x.rpm.*
3. To install the packed archives, change to the root directory of the web server and extract the package: *tar xzvf eGroupWare-x.x.x-x.tar.gz*
4. Next customize the rights for the eGroupWare files. The web server needs read and write rights in some folders, e.g. for *fudforum*.
5. In the next step ensure that the web server and the database are started, and start the browser.
6. Invoke the installation script from the browser: *http://server-adresse/egroupware/setup/*
7. The installations script will be started automatically at a correct installation. In the ideal case no error messages appear, and you reach header admin configuration (details to these steps are described in the following section).

8. Fill in every field here, download the file *header.inc.php* and save it in the root of the eGroupWare installation. In addition, grant the web server the right to be able to read the file and click on *Continue*.
9. Now log in into the system via the login.
10. Next create the required databases and tables. Fill in the user name and the corresponding password in the according form. Besides, a check up should be performed. Next the tables have to be created.
11. Next follows editing the current settings. Create a directory outside the web server root and permit the web server to read, write and execute it. If e.g. the web server root is in */var/www/html*, you could create the directory */var/www/dateien*.
12. In the next step create the user admin. Of course you shouldn't use this for the daily work with the system. He is designed exclusively for the administration.
13. In the second to the last step remove the applications which, for the time being, aren't needed. Now the system is in principle ready for use.

Since May 31st, 2004 eGroupWare is also available with a graphical Bitrock installer (www.bitrock.com). You do it like this:

1. In order to use it, first download the package *eGroupWare-1.0-install.bin*. After this open a terminal window and change the rights to make the package executable: *chmod 700 eGroupWare-1.0-install.bin*.
2. Then execute the setup wizard: *./eGroupWare-1.0-install.bin*
3. In its first dialogue the wizard welcomes users.
4. It is followed by the licence agreement, which you accept with *Yes*.
5. In the third dialogue determine the installation directory. The wizard recommends */var/www/html/*. If you use the XAMPP package, it would be a good idea to install eGroupWare in the directory */opt/lampp/htdocs/*.
6. Click on the button *Forward* to initialize the process of copying. A progression bar indicates this.
7. Finally the wizard indicates that the installation process is finished. Optionally the readme file may be displayed. It advises the user that now the browser may be started and that the installation script must be executed. The implementation of the system follows the above description.

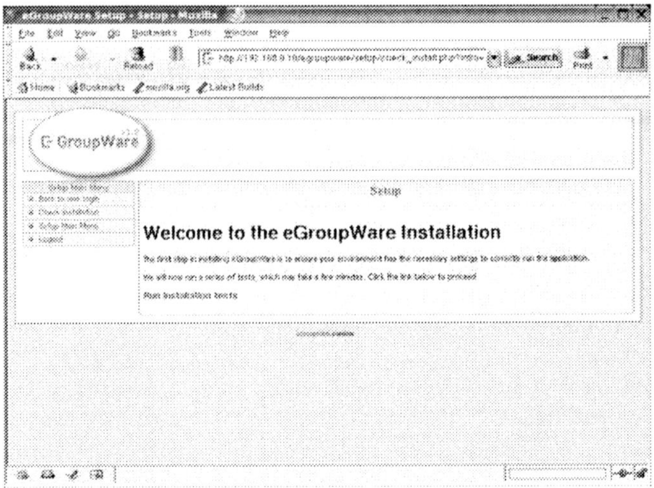

The setup wizard of eGroupWare after the call ot the URL *http://server-adresse/egroupware/setup/.*

8. The eGroupWare setup script welcomes the user. Now click on the link *Run installation tests*. Under certain conditions, the execution of the tests may need some time.
9. The test result indicates successful performed tests by a green hook. Failures are shown by a red cross and warnings by a yellow lightning.

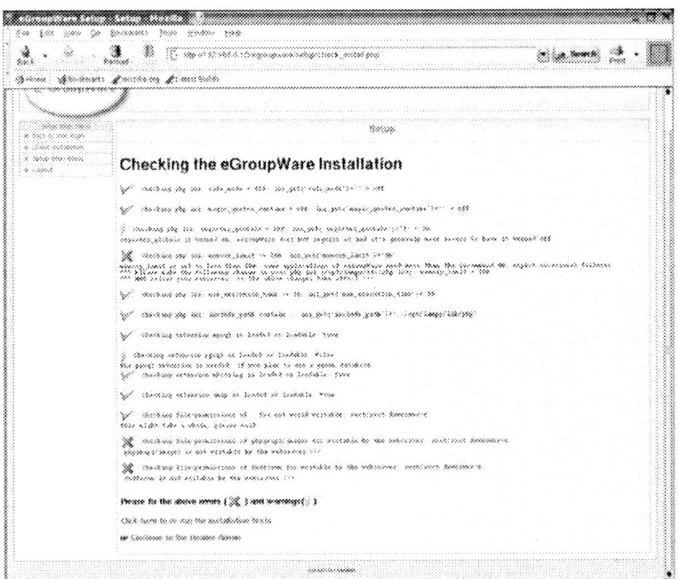

The test result of a first installation test. In this example, several rework is necessary to implement a properly functioning system.

10. In the testing result you will find hints how to solve each failure or warning. These flaws should be solved, and afterwards you should test the system again by clicking on the link *Click here to rerun the installation tests*.
11. In the test result there might appear a hint that the memory value of 8M allocated in the *php.ini* is to low and that instead the minimum value of 16M is necessary. In this case simply edit the file *php.ini* and adjust the value.
12. Another two sources of trouble: The authorizations for the directory */phpgwapi/images* and *fudforum* are not correct. This failure is also solved easily, e.g. by *chmod 700 images*.
13. After a restart of the Apache web server the test should be performed succesfully.
14. If all flaws are solved, click on the link *Continue to the Header Admin*.
15. In the following dialogue, it may be better to switch the language. In the dialogue *Setup* define the settings for the file *header.inc.php*. The dialogue first presents its analysis results, followed by the actual settings.
16. The actual settings are separated into two divisions. In the first you find the server root directory and include root (which should be the same directory as the server root). After this follow the settings for the admin user of the header managers and his password. In the following field enter the IP addresses or host names you want to restrict access to the setup. Besides you can decide whether you want to allow permanant database connection, and which session type (*php4* or *db*) should be used. The PHP4 session management provides a better performance. Next follow several MCrypt settings. On some Linux systems like e.g. SuSE linux there appear problems, indeed.

The setup wizard for the creation of the file *header.inc.php*.

17. In the second part define the domain name as well as the type of database (*MySQL* or *MS SQL Server*). Besides the following presettings must be edited:
    - Hostname/IP of the database server
    - TCP-Port of the database server
    - database name
    - database user
    - database password
    - configuration user
    - configuration password

    Of course it is important to deposit the passwords at another place because they will be encrypted and won't be accessable later on.
18. If the file *header.inc.php* cannot be created due to insuffiecient access rights, the setup allows downloading the file instead. Now you have to download the file *header.inc.php* and save it in the root directory of the eGroupWare installation. To do so, click on the button *Download*. After clicking on the button *Continue*, you reach a login dialogue, via which you obtain access to the system.
19. The setup dialogue presents two login dialogues: *Setup/Config Admin Login* and *Header Admin Login*. We follow the first, enter the before defined password, choose the desired language and click on *Login*.

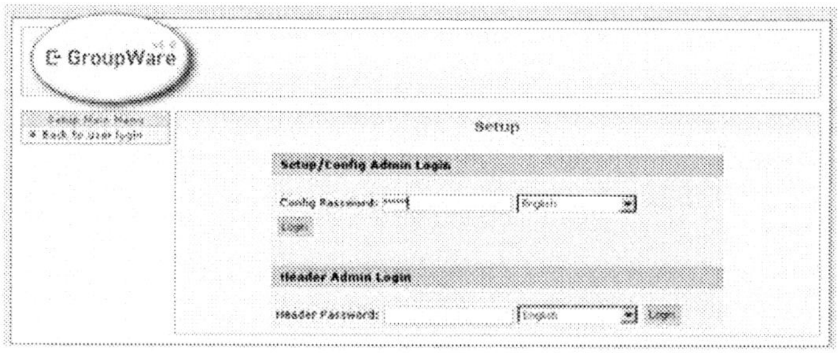

The Login for the creation of a database.

20. After the login eGroupWare presents another dialogue which helps you to create a simple application in only four steps. Each step which is not yet completed, will be indicated by a red cross. In the first step you create a database. To do so, enter the user name and the passwort of the database root server and then click on *Create Database*. It must be the same user name/password pair, as provided in the header.config.inc file.
21. Next follows a hint that the database has been created, but no application has been installed yet. Therefore click on *Install*, to set up all tables and the applications *Admin* and *Settings.*
22. After the system has managed this, a new click on *Check again* is necessary. The setup wizard finally reports the successful configuration. Also the language management and the advanced application management are completed succesfully.

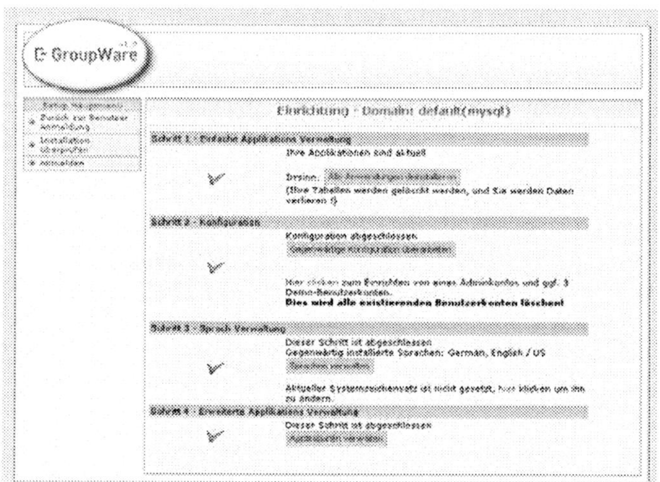

The setup is performed successfully.

23. To perform additional settings, click on *Edit current configuration.* These settings have to be edited, too, for eGroupWare to work.
24. In step 2 you find the link *Click here for admin account.* This step shouldnt't be omitted, and an according account should be set up.

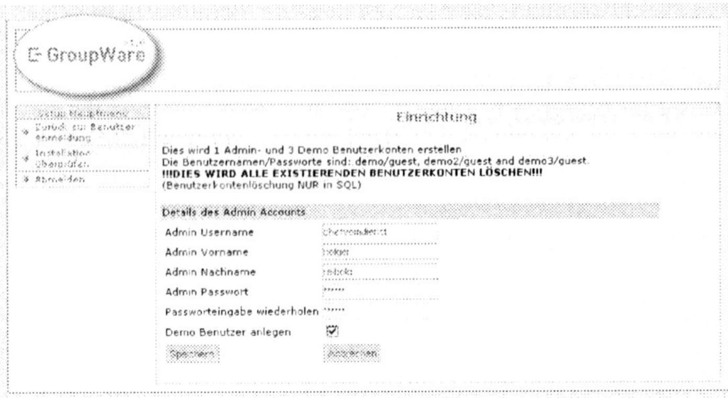

The setup of the admin account. It is possible to additionally set up miscallaneous demo users.

25. To log in to the system, just click on the link *Return to login,* or request the URL *http://system/egroupware/.* eGroupWare automaticallyopens the login dialogue, which now provides access to the system.

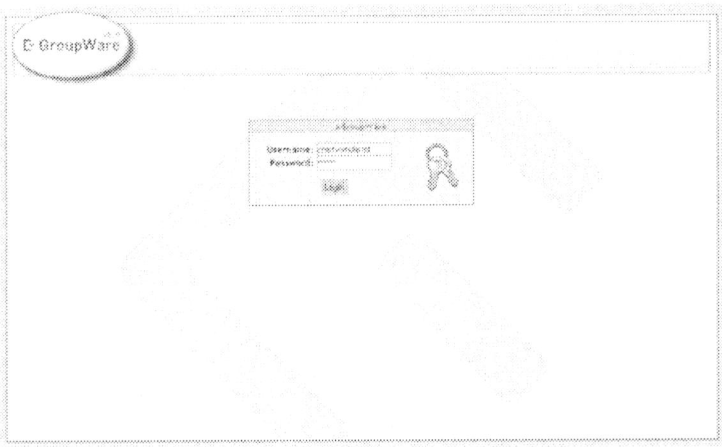

Congratulations – you managed it. Access to the system is gained via the login dialog.

2. Getting started with eGroupWare-Administration

After the first login, eGroupWare presents its typical interface. First of all the (still) empty calendar view stands out. In the left window area you find the different menues, over which you perform e.g. administrative tasks. The tool bar at the upper window area provides you access the typical Groupware functions like mail, calendar, address book etc.

The layout of the interface is always identical. Administrators and standard users are always presented the same layout: Above the tool bar, left the menues and below the tool bar the actual workspace. Common to all is the main menue, with which you get to the home page, access the individual settings, log off and access the menue info. Below the main menues you as the admin will find the admin menue. If e.g. you activate the calendar or the adsress book, the menue bar will be enhanced by the calendar menue and the calendar settings will be enlarged. It's similar with the other functions.

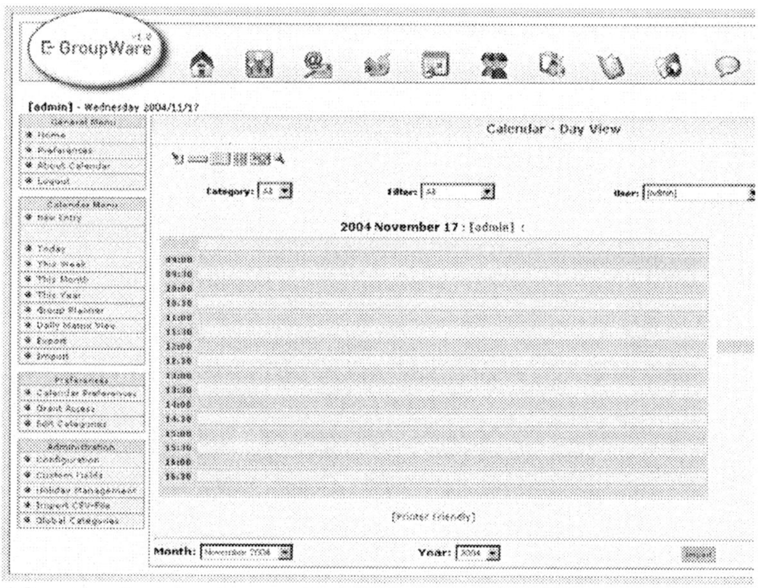

After the first log in as administrator eGroupWare presents it's typical interface.

Let's turn to the system administration. In order to open the administrative functions, you click after logging in as the administrator on the admin button of the tool bar. It's the very first icon from the left. Here you can configure the environment, set up user accounts and user groups, edit and delete applications, implement categories, display sessions, view protocols and so on.

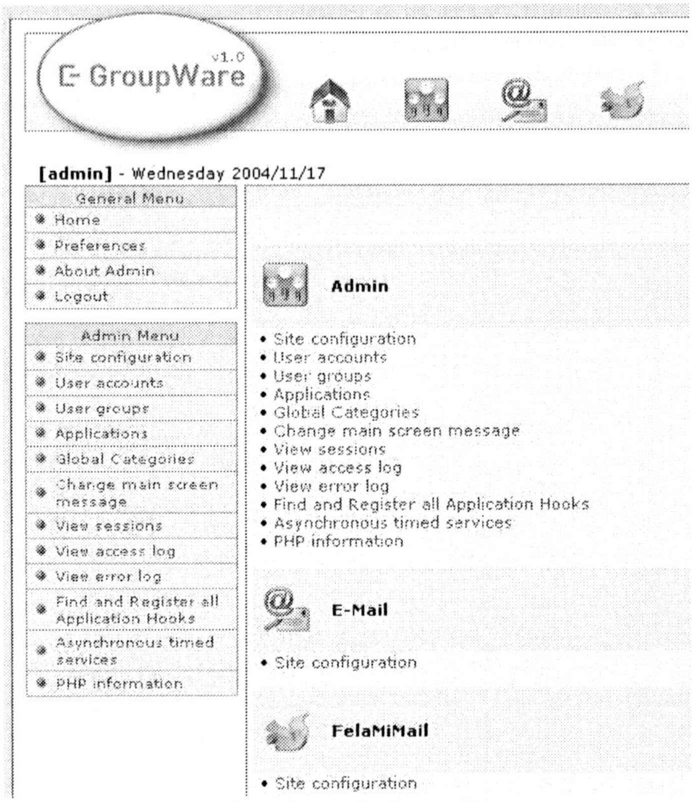

The administrative functions of eGroupWare.

If you click on the admin button, the admin menue in the left document area will also be opened. With this all administrative functions are available:

- Site configuration
- User accounts
- User groups
- Applications
- Global Categories
- Change main screen message
- View sessions
- View access log
- View error log
- Find and Register all Application Hooks
- Asynchronous times services
- PHP information

2.1 Site configuration

The link *Site configuration* lets you customize the configuration, the layout and the security related settings of eGroupWare. The according form divides the settings into the areas *Site configuration*, *Appearance* and *Security*.

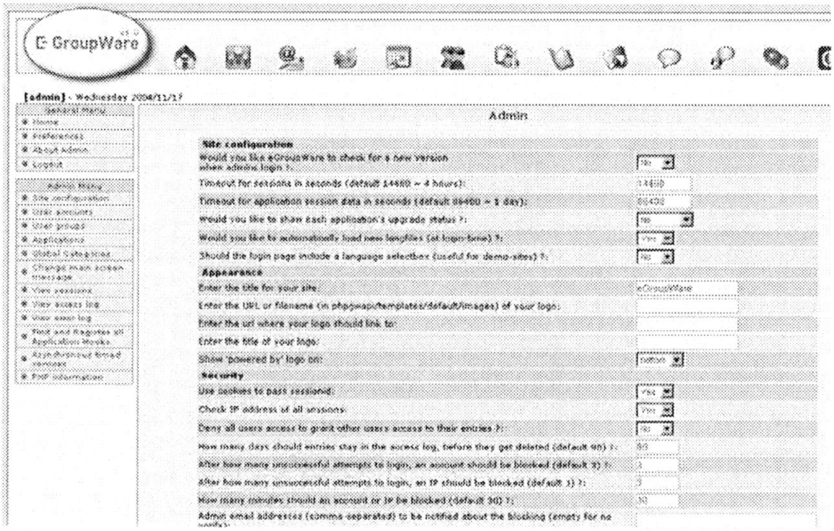

The configuration of the environment.

The settings for the configuration:

- **Would you like eGroupWare to check for a new version when admins login**: If you switch this setting to *Yes*, then at each login of an administrator a check will be performed wether there exists a newer version of eGroupWare. The default is *No* and can be maintained normally.
- **Timeout for sessions in seconds**: Here you define the length of time in seconds, after which a session will be invalid. The default value is 14400 (seconds, i.e. 4 hours).
- **Timeout for application session data in seconds**: Here you define after which period of time the session data of an application will be deleted. The default value is 86400 seconds, i.e. one day.
- **Would you like to automatically load new langfiles**: If you choose *Yes*, at each log in a check will be performed whether new languages are available. This option should normally be deactivated and only be activated if needed (in order to save system ressources). The automatical loading of languages is only suitable for small installations. As for large systems you should update this manually in the setup.

Following are the settings for the layout of the eGroupWare-installation:

- **Enter the title for your site:** Here you find the title which e.g. is displayed in the title bar of the browser. At use in the enterprise, you for example, could type in the company name here.

- **Enter the URL or filename (in phpgwapi/templates/default/images) of your logo:** Here you fill in the filename of your logo.
- **Enter the url where your logo should link to**: In this field you indicate the URL to which one will get if one clicks on the logo in the left upper edge.
- **Show 'powered by' logo on**: With this select menue you determine whether the powered by hint will be shown at the bottom or at the top of the page.

Following are the security settings with their options:

- **Use cookies to pass sessionid**: This setting should be set on *Yes*, because the session should be passed in a cookie by all means.
- **Check IP address of all sessions**: With this option the so called session hijacking can be eliminated. For this purpose it will be checked whether the session is used by the same IP. But it does not grasp if the attacker is on the way in the same network. The default is *Yes*.
- **Deny all users access to grant other users access to their entries?**: If this feature is set to *Yes*, a user can not anymore gain access to his data by himself. The access management will then be overtaken by administrators. Here the default is *No*.
- **How many days should entries stay in the access log, before they get deleted?**: Here you determine how many time entries should be saved in the access log. The default 90 days should be maintained. Lower values do not lead to performance benefits.
- **After how many unsuccessful attempts to login, an account should be blocked?**: Here you define how often a user may unseccessfully try until his account will blocked. The default *3* has been aproven in the practise.
- **After how many unsuccessful attempts to login, an IP should be blocked?:** This function fulfills the same task as the above mentioned. The only difference: One uses an IP address. The default is here 3 as well.
- **How many minutes should an account or IP be blocked?** If an account is blocked e.g. due to unsuccessful logins, it will be unblocked after the period of time defined here. The default is 30 minutes.
- **Admin email addresses (comma-separated) to be notified about the blocking**: Here you determine the email address(es) of the administrator(s) who will be informed about a blocking.
- **Disable „auto completion“ of the login form**: Finally the auto completion of the login data can be switched off. If you choose *Yes*, the browser does not try to save the account information. Dependant on the environment and the range of use it is recommended to switch off this function.

2.2 User accounts

If you click on the link *User accounts*, you get to eGroupWare user management. Here you find beside the administrator three further demo users (as far as you have agreed to create them during the installation). Any user who wants to use the system needs an account of its own. In the user view all the users that are quite created are listed including the login ID and first name and last name. Besides the user settings can be edited, deleted (of course not the admin account) and displayed.

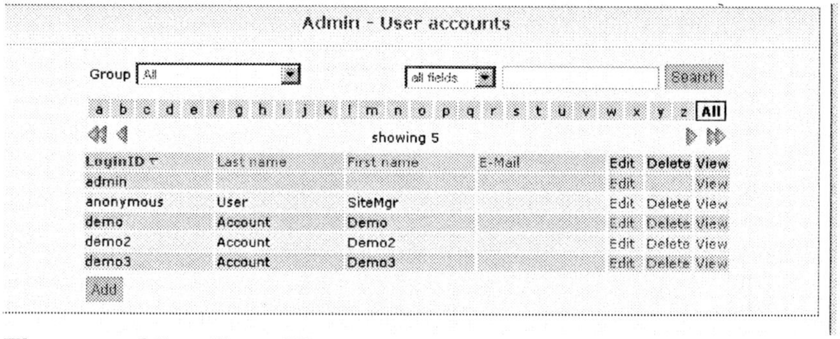

The users of the eGroupWare system.

With the button *Add* you can create new users. The according dialogue *Add new account* complies with the dialogue to edit an account except for one difference: It still does not show the link *ACL Rights*. This is quite natural, because it still is not created or saved nor provided with access rights. The view by the way opens a tabulated overview of the user settings. Editing is not possible here. Let us have a closer look at the settings of a demo user. Therefore we click on the entry *demo* in the user list.

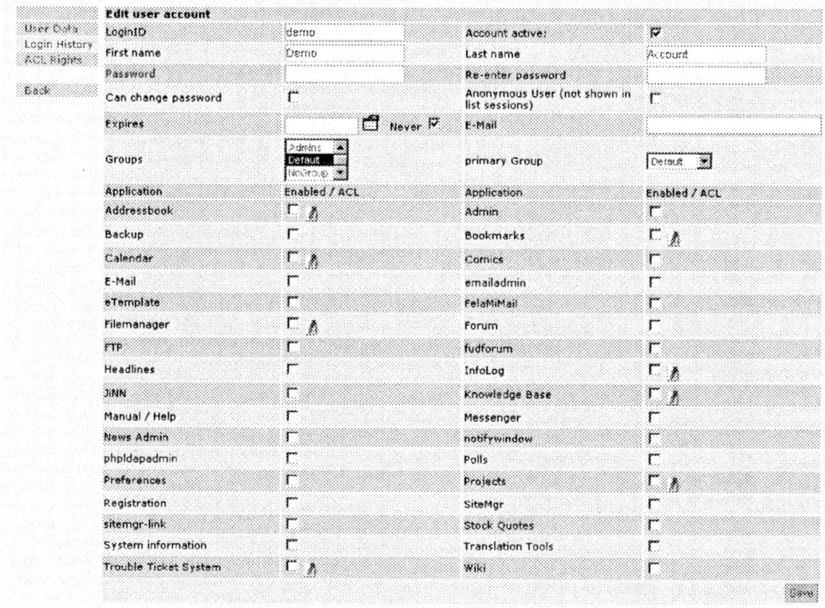

Editing a demo user.

By default, when editing the user settings the form *Edit user account* will be opened. Here the information about the user can be put in and edited. The following settings are available:

- **LoginID**: The user name for the account.
- **Account active**: Here you determine whether the account is activated or deactivated. If an account is deactivated, the user can not log in.
- **First name**: First name of the user.
- **Last name**: Last name of the user.
- **Password**: Password for the account.
- **Re-enter password**: Here you repeat the entered password. Thus you must assure that you have not mistyped by the first input.
- **Can change password**: Determines whether the user is allowed to change his password or not.
- **Anonymous User**: Defines whether anonymus users are shown under V*iew sessions* or not.
- **Expires**: Here a date of expiration can be defined for the user account. If the account should not expire, activate the check box *Never*.
- **Groups**: Here you determine to which group(s) the user belongs.
- **primary Group**: In this select menu you determine the primary user group.

Further check boxes will follow, e.g. for the address book, file manager, and so on. They serve for enabling applications to the particuar user. It is recommended, to control these authorizations by the group membership. With the user management there are two additional forms available: *Login History* and *ACL Rights*. Under *Login History* the last sessions of the user are displayed. A table itemizes when a user had logged in with which IP address. With *ACL Rights* you can manage the ACL rights of the user. But you can only withdraw the user rights in the admin application by this form.

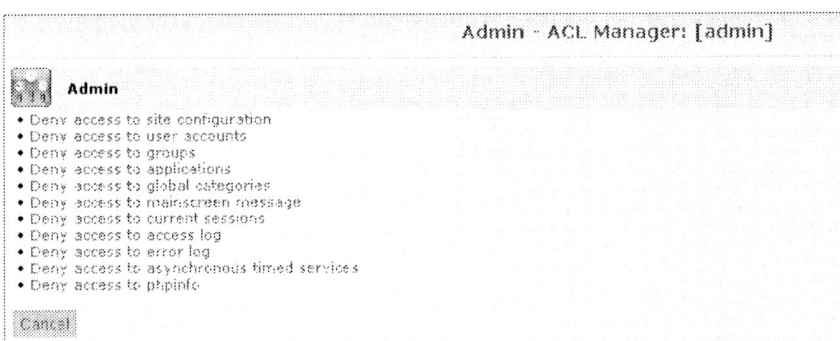

The form *ACL Rights*.

2.3 User groups

In the user groups you collect the users. This makes the user administration easier quite considerably, because you can create superior categories with the according authorizations. Users who match a certain profile are just put in such a directory.

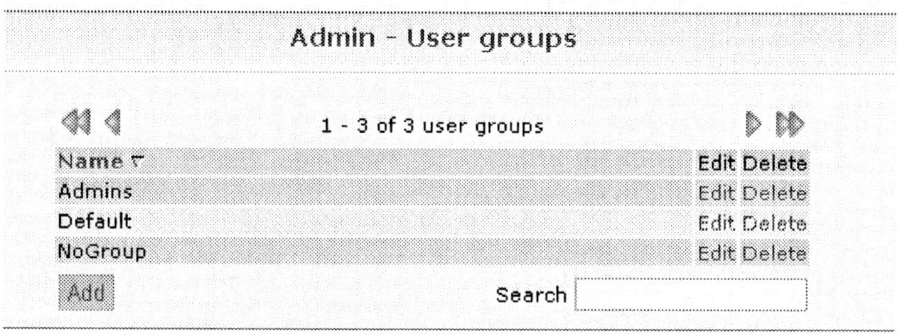

The user group management.

In the user group managment you find after a standard installation the two groups *Admins* and *Default.* With the link *Edit* you can edit the group preferences, and with the button *Delete* it can be deleted. Besides, as also in the user management, there's a search function available, that enables you to browse the group management.

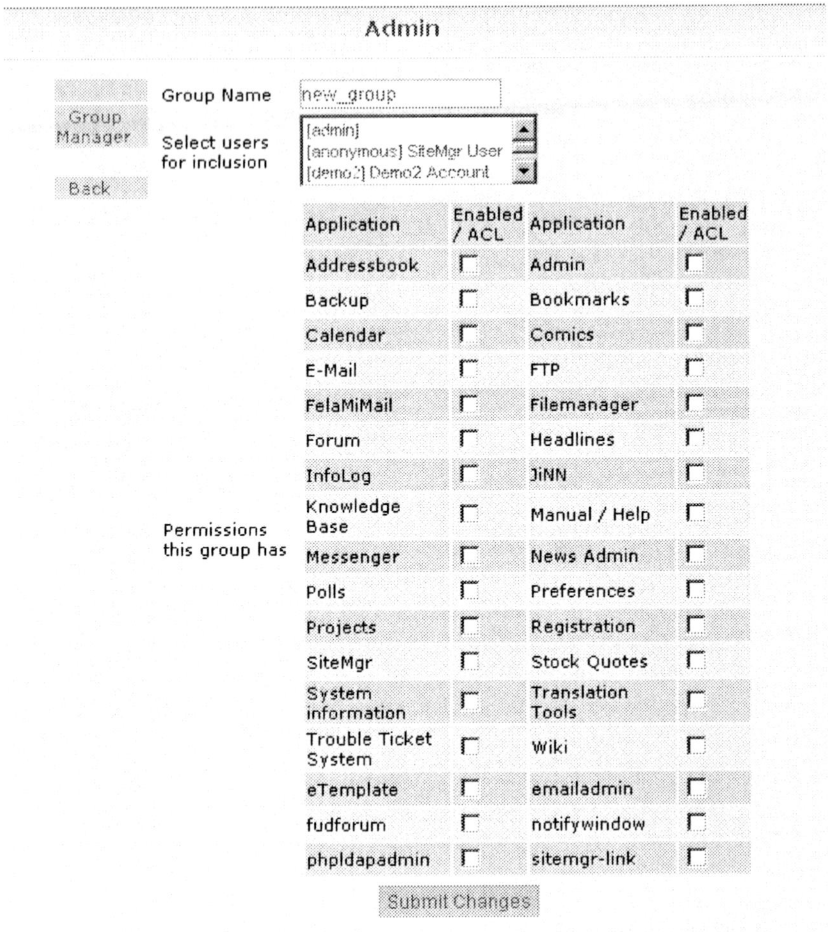

A new user groups arises.

To add a new group, you click on the button *Add.* In the appropriate document you fill in the settings for the new group. There are three preferences to set: defining the group name, selecting the users, and determining the access rights. The settings in detail:

- **Group Name**: In this input field you determine the name of the group.
- **Select users for inclusion**: With this selection dialogue you can select the users that should be members of the group. If they are not created, any users that should be members of this group, can assign the users directly when creating the group.
- **Permissions this group has**: Here you determine the applications the users of this group may access. If users are members of different groups, the applications are collected. If e.g. user is a member of two groups that both have access to the calendar, the user has also acces to to calendar. If one of the groups does not have access to the calendar, the user also has access to it, because the other group provides access to the calendar. Be-

sides access rights can be assigned on user level. ACL rights cannot be assigned here yet. This must be edited in the group later on.

With the form *Group Manager* you can in the future define one user or even several users as manager(s) for the group. If you click at the bottom edge of the document on the button *Submit Changes*, the new group will be created, and you now get to the group list view, which now also lists the new group.

2.4 Applications

With the link *Applications* you get to the preferences of the installed eGroupWare applications. The according dialogue itemies the available applications including status. As for the other dialogues, the green arrows indicate that there are further pages available. Of course they allow to navigate between these pages.

As known from the above forms, editing and deleting of the applications is possible. Before the deletion security request will be performed, whether the planned step really shall be carried out. If you want to use new applications that are not mentioned here, you click on the link *Setup*, which will open the login form for the eGroupWare setup.

Admin - Installed applications

showing 1 - 15 of 34

Title	Edit	Delete	Enabled
Addressbook	Edit	Delete	Yes
Admin	Edit	Delete	Yes
Backup	Edit	Delete	Yes
Bookmarks	Edit	Delete	Yes
Calendar	Edit	Delete	Yes
Comics	Edit	Delete	Yes
E-Mail	Edit	Delete	Yes
emailadmin	Edit	Delete	Yes
eTemplate	Edit	Delete	Yes
FelaMiMail	Edit	Delete	Yes
Filemanager	Edit	Delete	Yes
Forum	Edit	Delete	Yes
FTP	Edit	Delete	Yes
fudforum	Edit	Delete	Yes
Headlines	Edit	Delete	Yes

Add (To install new applications use Setup [Manage Applications] !!!)

The alphabetical list of the installed eGroupWare applications.

The edit dialogues of all applications look identical. They list the name of the application and allow editing the state. The following options are available:

- Disabled

- Enabled
- Enabled – Hidden from nav bar
- Enabled – Popup Window

Besides the position of the application in the navigation bar can be customized. The higher the value, the more rightwards the application will be shown. The value 1 means left-most position. With the button *Save* you accept the changes.

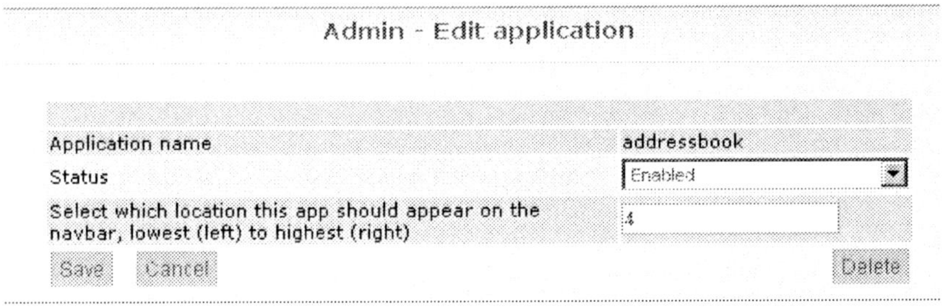

Editing the application preferences.

2.5 Global Categories

The function *Global Categories* helps you to manage the data in eGroupWare more efficient. Most of the applications in eGroupWare support global categories. So you can e.g. create a global category for each department of a company. It is possible to show all entries of a categorie in the address book. The advantage: You find the desired information fast, e.g. without having to use the search function.

eGroupWare also supports subcategories, in which then e.g. internal information or information of the marketing department, the distribution department and the development department are deposited. In the ideal case you think about the implementation of such categories in the beginning of the installation. The subsequent implementation of such hierarchies is rather problematical, because the data must be inserted into the categories manually.

Creating a global category is easy. After you have clicked on *Add* in the categoriy view, you get to a form in which you type in a superior category, the name and a description. If there some categories already exist, you can also create subcategries by the option *Add sub*. Similarly easy is the deletion of global categories. To do so, you simply click on *Delete* beneath the category in the categories view and confirm the deletion process in the next dialogue.

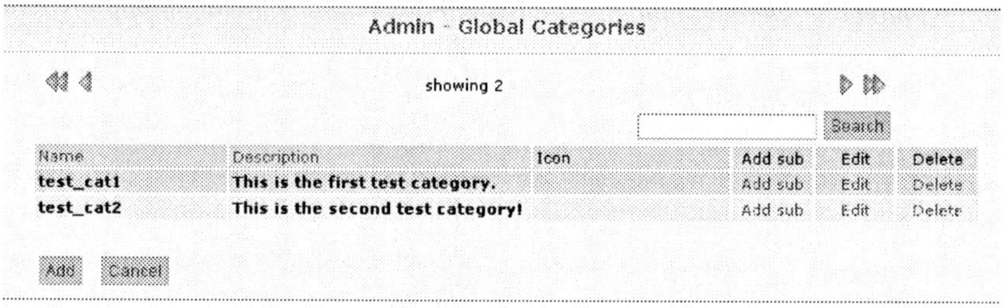

The management of the global categories.

Important in this context: If you delete a category, the associated data records will not be deleted. However, it has to be taken into account when deleting, that if one deletes a category with sub-categories, the sub-categories can be deleted as well or can continue to exist. If you do not delete the sub-categories as well, they will rise in rank one step. If the deleted category is not a sub-category of another, they remain categories of the first level.

2.6 Change main screen message

The functions of the link *Change main screen message* are not very spectacular. With the according form you can edit the message text that should be displayed after the login. Also the text of the login page can be edited. For both pages you can fill in separate text in English or another language.

Editing is easy. With the select menu you first choose the start or login page and then you click on *Edit* to open the edit field, in which you type in the message text. This will be displayed after the next system start. But you should keep in mind that this message will not be displayed after the login, if you define another page as start page, e.g. the calendar. These preferences are available on the main menu.

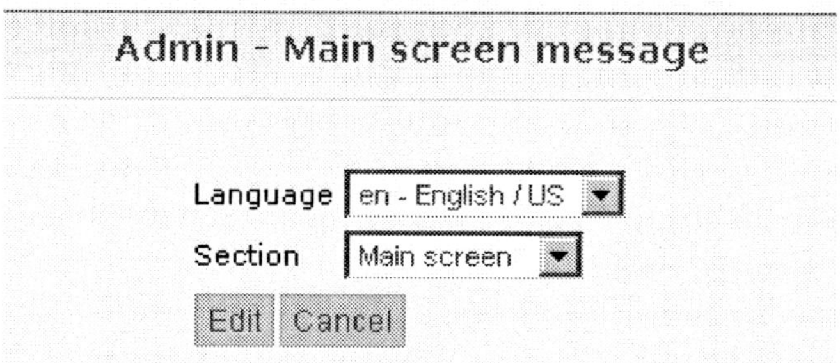

Customizing the main screen.

2.7 View sessions

With the page *View sessions* information will be displayed about the actual open sessions. Beside the login names also the login time, the last action and the idle time of the user are listed. If a user logs off invalid, the sessions will not be closed and will still be continued. In such a case you should close the session by the link *Kill.*

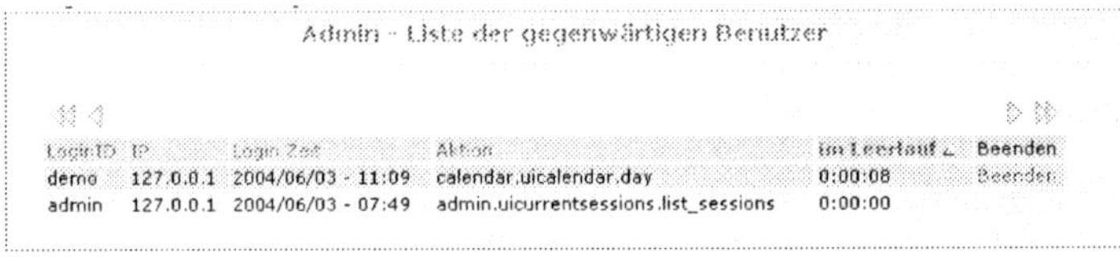
Admin - Liste der gegenwärtigen Benutzer

LoginID	IP	Login Zeit	Aktion	im Leerlauf	Beenden
demo	127.0.0.1	2004/06/03 - 11:09	calendar.uicalendar.day	0:00:08	Beenden
admin	127.0.0.1	2004/06/03 - 07:49	admin.uicurrentsessions.list_sessions	0:00:00	

The session view of eGroupWare.

2.8 View access log

eGroupWare has several protocol functions that provide the administrator with valuable information about utilization, usage and errors of the environment. With the link *View access log* of the admin menu the access logs are available.

A table itemizes user name, IP address, date and time of each attempt to login. Also the logout date is indicated here. The document also shows the percentage of useres that have logged in correctly.

As the administrator you should have a look at the access log from time to time. Especially because also the failed login attempts are listed here. You will get a quick overview about potential attacks and can take first steps against them and e.g. block the IP address of the aggressor.

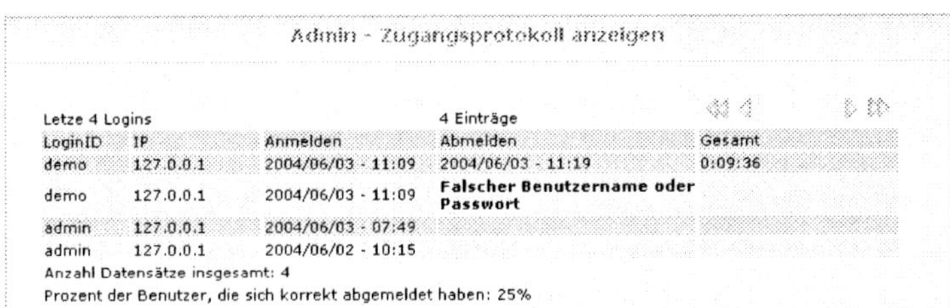
Admin - Zugangsprotokoll anzeigen

Letze 4 Logins — 4 Einträge

LoginID	IP	Anmelden	Abmelden	Gesamt
demo	127.0.0.1	2004/06/03 - 11:09	2004/06/03 - 11:19	0:09:36
demo	127.0.0.1	2004/06/03 - 11:09	**Falscher Benutzername oder Passwort**	
admin	127.0.0.1	2004/06/03 - 07:49		
admin	127.0.0.1	2004/06/02 - 10:15		

Anzahl Datensätze insgesamt: 4

Prozent der Benutzer, die sich korrekt abgemeldet haben: 25%

A simple example of an access log.

2.9 View error log

In the document *View error log* all errors are itemized that have occurred while performing the script. As for most of the users and administrators these errors are not that interesting. Unlike developers, who e.g. have written their own modules. But also the experienced administrator can track possible flaws by the error messages that are available here.

The entries describe in which file and in which line the error occured. This information helps the developer to localize the problem. The layout of the table can be customized.

2.10 Find and Register all Application Hooks

The function with the curious title *Find and Register all Application Hooks* simply lists the entries, which are also listed by clicking on the *Admin* icon in the tool bar. Developers may use it to check whether the new application is displayed as designated.

But this function is also interesting for administrators. They can use it after an update to make the most recent update of an eGroupWare module available without having to invoke the setup or login new.

2.11 Asynchronous timed services

The functions of the link *Asynchronous timed services* are more interesting. The asynchronous timed services are a very useful feature of eGroupWare, which e.g. lets you send emails even if a user is not logged in. After the installation only the option *fallback (after each pageview)* is available. What does this mean? An example: If you e.g. set a mail alarm for a certain date, a mail will be sent as soon as a user takes an action in eGroupWare. If this alarm mail should be sent to a date at which no eGroupWare user is logged in, the mail will not be sent automatically. To solve this roblem, a cron job is used.

You do it like this: You create an entry in the cron table that defines how often the corresponding PHP script should be invoked. The cron service regularly looks up if a program has to be started. If yes, it will be invoked.

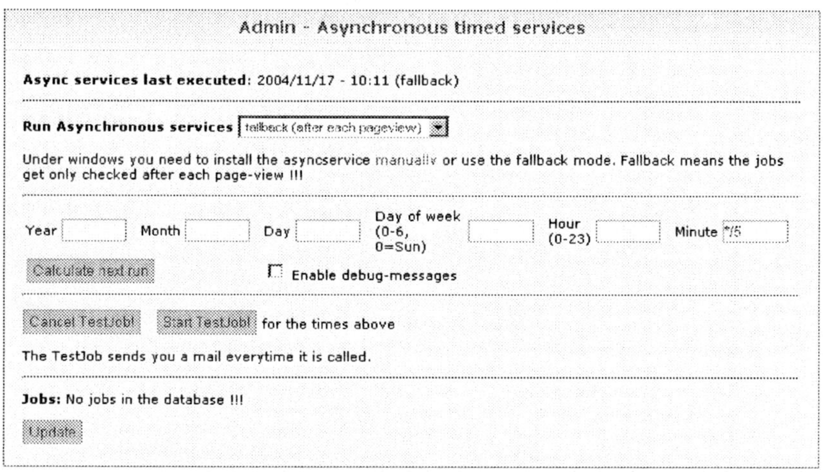

The function *Asynchronous timed services.*

In order to use a crontab entry with eGroupWare, you need the necessary rights on the server. If this is possible, the service can be configred as follows: First you define the desired date. If the planned action shall be performed in intervals, you only need to fill out the input filed *Minute*. The value **/15* e.g. checks every 15 minutes, whether a task has to be performed. Then you click on *Install crontab*. To test the functionality of the service, you use the button *Start TestJob!*

2.12 PHP information

The link *PHP information* displays information about the PHP environment. The information shown here is generated by a phpinfo() call. This presents the options set in the file *php.ini*.

2.13 Configuring applications

As the administrator and the users can use the different applications they must be confgured by the system administrator. Only now the individual users can configure their environment in order to e.g. send mails or use addresses on a directory server.

In order to configure the applications, the administrator clicks on the button *Admin* in the tool bar. Beneath the above described admin preferences you find a standard installation of links for the configuration of the Email, Calendar, Addressbook, InfoLog, Headlines and Bookmark services.

2.14 Configuring Email

With the Email preferences you configure eGroupWare for the teamwork with the POP3/IMAP4 and the SMTP server. Whereas mails are fetched from a POP/IMAP server, a SMTP server serves the dispatch. This doesn't have to be local servers. You can also use the servers of a provider, as long as the machine running the eGroupWare system is permanently (at least during the usual working hours) connected to the internet.

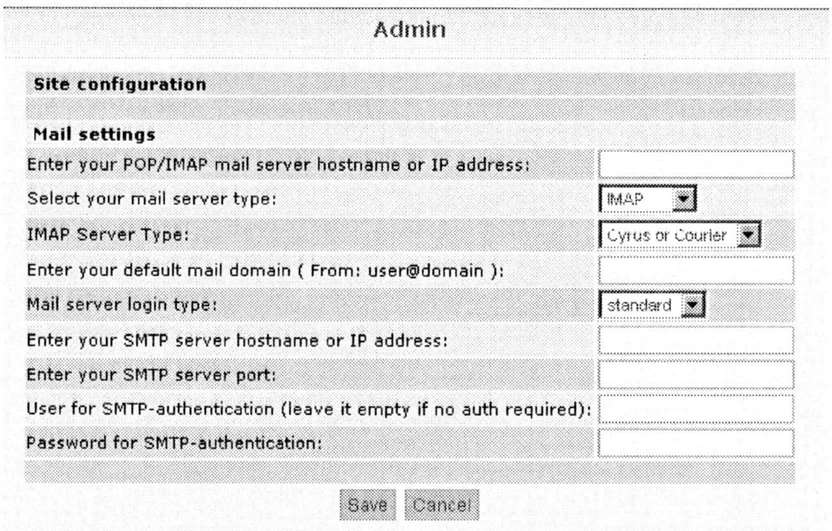

The configuration of the Email service.

The settings in detail:

- **Enter your POP/IMAP mail server hostname or IP address:** Here you fill in the host names respectively the IP address of the POP/IMAP server, that is used locally or on the part of the provider.
- **Select your mail server type:** With this select menu you define whether it is a POP3 or an IMAP4 server resp. a secure variant.
- **IMAP Server Type**: If an IMAP server is used, you select the type. The following types are selectable: *Cyrus or Courier*, *UWash,* and *UW-Maildir*.
- **Enter your default mail domain (From: user@domain):** In this input field you type in the standard domain.
- **Mail server login type**: In this select menu you determine the login type. Selectable are *standard* and *vmailmgr*. As a general rule the option *standard* is used. *vmailmgr* (Virtual MAIL ManaGeR) is a collection of programs to administrate multiple daemons and mailboxes on one host. Details are available on *www.vmailmgr.org*.
- **Enter your SMTP server hostname or IP address**: Here you fill in the host name resp. the IP address of the SMTP server.
- **Enter your SMTP server port**: Here you determine the port of the SMTP server. The default is 25.

With the button *Save* you save the changes made and get back to the admin overview.

2.15 Configuring Calendar

There are several settings available for the configuration of the calendar functions. Beneath the actual settings, you can implement user defined fields and edit the sorting, manage holidays, import CSV files and acess the settings for the global categories.

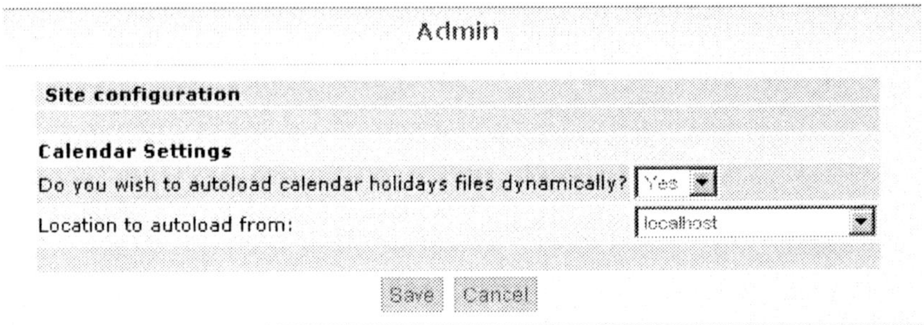

The calendar settings.

With the link *Site configuration* a simple form opens, by which you only can make changes for the holiday specific settings:

- **Do you wish to autoload calendar holidays files dynamically?** Here you define whether the information shall be obtained automatically or not. The default setting is *No*.
- **Location to autoload from**: If you decide *Yes*, you can define by this select menu, whether they should be obtained from *localhost* or via *www.egroupware.org*.

The preferences that hide behind the link *Custom fields and sorting* are very flexible. Here you define the preferences for the forms that will be opened by clicking on a time, a day and so on in the calendar view. It is a form for creating a new calendar entry.

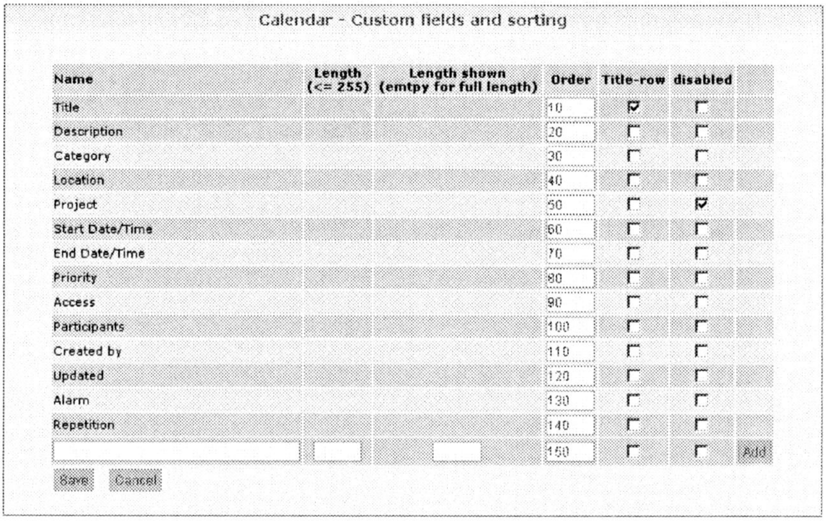

The configuration of the form for creating a new calendar entry.

For each input field the name, length of the input feld, length shown, order, title-row and switching are displayed. If you want to implement additional fields, you use the last line of the form, name the field and define the properties. With the button *Add*, the input form will be enhanced accordingly and will then be available for the users.

With the link *Calendar Holiday Management*, you open the so called holiday management. The appropriate document itemizes the holidays. With the button *Add* you can enhance the current setting by additional entries. In the form *Add Holiday* you put in the country, the title of the day, the date and the occurence.

The calendar function allows importing a CSV file (Comma separated values) for the link *Import CSV-File*. A CSV file is a normal text file, where in the separate lines several data are saved. Here you choose the file, the fieldseparator (mostly a comma), and the charset that is to be used. With this function you can especially import information that conforms to ICalendar resp. vCalendar. Finally the calendar function allows direct access to the global categries (see above).

2.16 Configuring Addressbook

Also the addressbook needs to be configurated for the corporation-wide use. With the according dialogue you especially make changes to several LDAP specific preferences. To do so, you need appropriate information about the LDAP server configuration. The preferences in detail:

- **Select where you want to store/retrieve contacts**: Here you define whether the contacts are drawn from/saved on a SQL database or a LDAP server.
- **LDAP host for contacts**: Here you put in the host name resp. the IP address of the LDAP server.

- **LDAP context for contacts**: Here you define the so called contexts.
- **LDAP root dn for contacts**: The entry *root dn* is the distinct name for a user who is not enforced on restrictions on parameters for the acess control or user management for maintaining LDAP directories. The user *rootdn* is in a manner of speaking root of the LDAP directory.
- **LDAP root pw for contacts**: Here you finally put in the password.

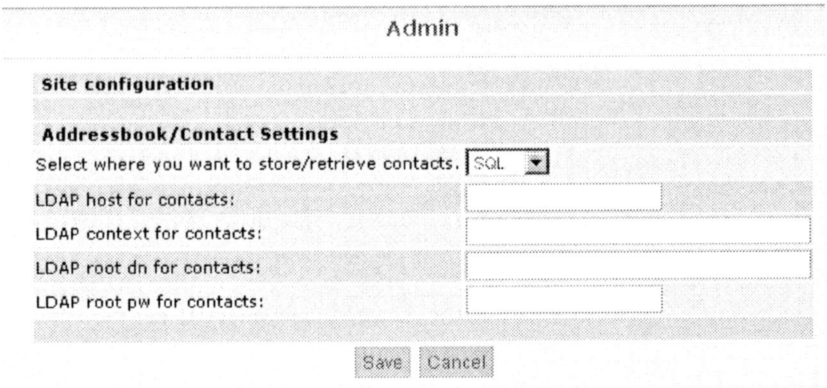

The configuration of the adressbook.

In the configuration of the addressbook you can also add user defined fields and global categories. The functionality has been described above.

2.17 Configuring InfoLog

InfoLog is a CRM tool that uses the adressbook functionality in order to create task lists, notes and telephone protocols. By the use of this tool typical actions can be performed, e.g. delegating tasks. Besides it is possible to protocol all activities of a contact or project. The program furthermore allows linking of files and documents and the CSV import.

Interesting additions are planned for the future. It shall be possible to deliver Email notification for new tasks and integrate facsimile into the program. With the according form you determine the path to the common filing and to the web server. The InfoLog configuration furthermore allows editing the global categories, fields, types and status as well as CSV import.

2.18 Configuring Headlines

The module *Headliines* allows the users to display seleced newsfeeds in their client. Newsfeeds are short summaries of news. Different web pages offer such newsfeeds, e.g. KDE News, LinuxToday, Mozilla News and Slashdot. With this dialogue you determine which Newsfeeds the users can use. The headline management already supplies a good collection of such offers. According to customs, the entries can be edited, deleted or even just displayed.

The confguration of the newsfeeds.

With the link *Edit* you access the feed settings. There you can edit the name, the base URL, the path to the RDF file, the period of time for actualization in minutes, the number of headlines and the news type. If you are interested in further news, you simply click on *Grab new news sites*. The system will display a large list then.

2.19 Configuring bookmarks

Finally in the admin menu the bookmarks preferences are available. Here you especially define, which text hint should be added when sending bookmarks to other users. In the bookmark settings you can also access the global categories.

2.20 Subsequent changes of the system confguration

As seen at the end of the first chapter, the configuration of eGroupWare is done with the URL *machinename/egroupware/setup/*. The appropriate form provides the two logins *Setup/Config Admin Login* and *Header Admin Login*. Both enable you to edit the preferences of the environment afterwards. In doing so, you must be very careful, because existing configurations are overwritten by changes.

After logging in with *Setup/Config Admin Login* eGroupWare presents the dialogue we already became acquainted with above, that serves the setup of the domain by its five steps. This dialogue provides further setting options for customizing the system. It first displays in its headline the site name and the database system used.

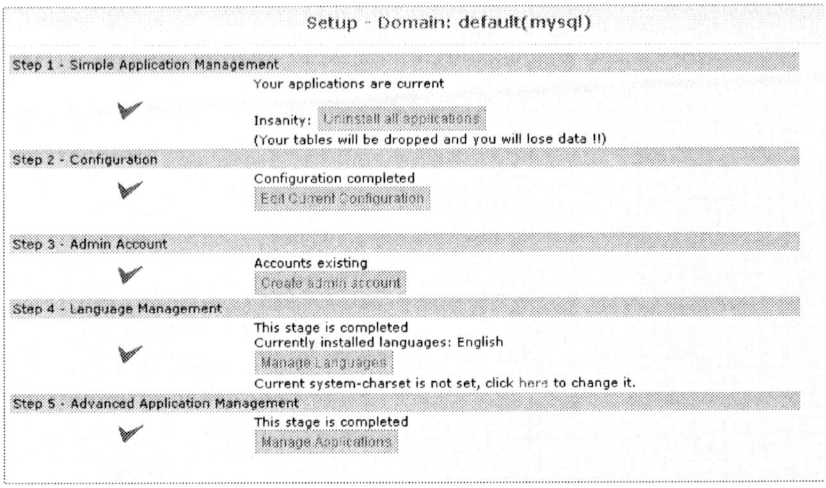

The dialogue after logging in with the *Setup/Config Admin Login.*

Step 1 serves for the application management. With the button *Uninstall all applications* they will be removed from the system. You should really avoid this step, because the tables will be deleted and the data will be lost hereby. Besides the document displays the application status, e.g. *Your applications are current.*

With step 2 you can edit the current configuration. If the system is functioning properly, the status report *Configuration completed* will be displayed here. With the button *Edit Current Configuration* a large dialogue opens that lets you make a lot of changes.

Let us have a look at the functions for editing the current configuration. The appropriate form summarizes the settings into five groups: *Path information, Host information, Authentication / Accounts, MCrypt Settings* and *Additional settings.*

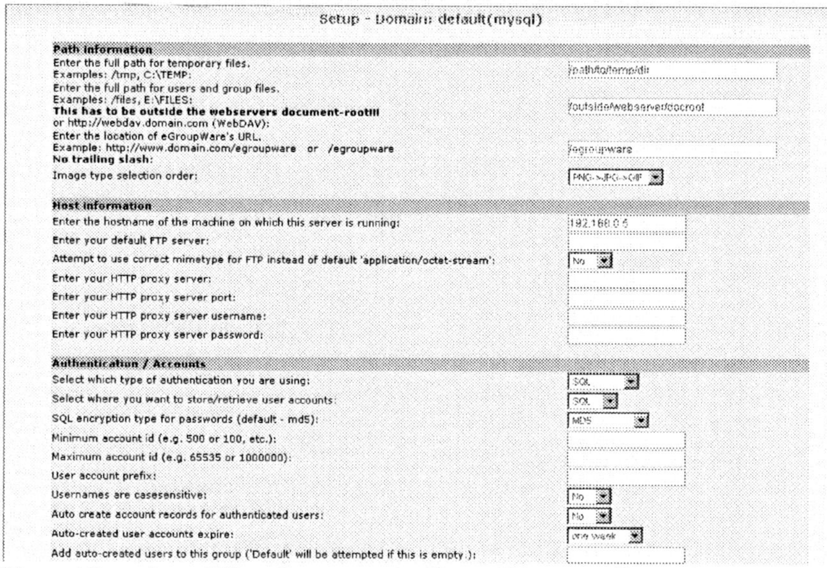

The settings for editing the current eGroupWare configuration.

In the field *Path information* you edit the following preferences:

- **Enter the full path for temporary files**: Here you fill in the path for the temporary files, e.g. */tmp* or *C:\TEMP*:
- **Enter the full path for users and group files.**: Here you define the path to the user and group file, e.g. */files* or *E:\Files*. Important here: The path must be outside webserver document-root. If you use WebDAV, you also can define a URL in the form of *http://webdav.domain.com.*
- **Enter the location of eGroupWare's URL**: Here you determine the the standard URL to the eGroupware installation. With the standard installation it reads *machinename/egroupware*. It is important that you do not use a trailing slash.
- **Image type selection order**: With the last select menu of the path preferences you finally define the order in which the system accesses graphics. There are three options available: *Standard GIF-JPG-PNG*, *PNG-JPG-GIF* and *PNG-JPG.*

Following are the host specific preferences. The settings in detail:

- **Enter the hostname of the machine on which this server is running**: Here you put in the host name of the machine the eGroupWare installation is running on. The default is *localhost.*
- **Enter your default FTP server**: In this input field you type in the host name resp. default FTP server.
- **Attempt to use correct mimetype for FTP instead of default 'application/octet-stream'**: Here you have the choice between the default setting *No* and *Yes*. The default should be maintained.

- **Enter your HTTP proxy server**: eGroupWare also colaborates with proxy servers. In this field you fill in the address resp. the host name of the proxy server.
- **Enter your HTTP proxy server port**: Here you type in the port of the proxy.
- **Enter your HTTP proxy server username**: If a username is necessary for using the proxy server, you type it into this input field.
- **Enter your HTTP proxy server password**: In this field type the password if necessary.

Following are the preferences for the authentication and the user accounts. The following configuration preferences are available here:

- **Select which type of authentication you are using**: With this selection field you define the authentication type. The following are selectable: *SQL*, *SQL/SSL*, *LDAP*, *Mail*, *HTTP* and *NIS*.
- **Select where you want to store/retrieve user accounts**: Here too, you can select between two options, and that are *SQL* and *LDAP*.
- **Minimum account id (e.g. 500 or 100, etc.):** With the following input field you define the minimum amount of user IDs.
- **Maximum account id (e.g. 65535 or 1000000):** Here you limit the possible amount.
- **Auto create account records for authenticated users**: Here you select whether accounts for authenticated users shuld be created autmatically. This switch is set on *Yes* by default.
- **Auto-created user accounts expire**: With this select menu you define whether auto created accounts should expire after one or two weeks, after one month or never.
- **Add auto-created users to this group ('Default' will be attempted if this is empty.):** Here you fill in the group name that should be added to the auto created user.
- **If no ACL records for user or any group the user is a member of**: With this select menu you define whether access should be granted for a user or a group resp. denied, if there is no according ACL entry.

If eGroupWare uses LDAP, there are also a lot of preferences available.

- **Do you want to manage homedirectory and loginshell attributes?**
- **LDAP Default homedirectory prefix**
- **LDAP Default shell**
- **LDAP host**
- **LDAP accounts context**
- **LDAP search filter for accounts, default**
- **LDAP groups context**
- **LDAP rootdn (searching accounts and changing passwords)**
- **LDAP root password**
- **LDAP encryption type**
- **Enable LDAP Version 3**

Following are the MCrypt preferences. In order to use them, the PHP mcrypt enhancement is necessary. The following preferences can be set:

- **Enter some random text for app session encryption:**
- **Mcrypt algorithm (default TRIPLEDES)**
- **Mcrypt mode (default CBC)**

Finally another two preferences are available.

- **Select where you want to store/retrieve filesystem information**: Here you define whether you want to store or retrieve file information like file type, size, version etc. via SQL or via WebDAV.
- **Select where you want to store/retrieve file contents**: With the last select menu you define whether you want to retrieve or store the file contents to/from the file system or to/from a SQL database. The developers recommend the option *File system.*

The third step provides the link *Create admin account*. You should be very careful here, because executing it will delete all existing user accounts.

With the fourth step, the so called language management takes place. As for the steps above, a status report is also given out here, e.g. the message *Currently installed languages: German, English/US*. In order to customize the language preferences, you click on *Manage Languages*. With the appropriate dialogue the multilingual support can be customized resp. new languages can be installed.

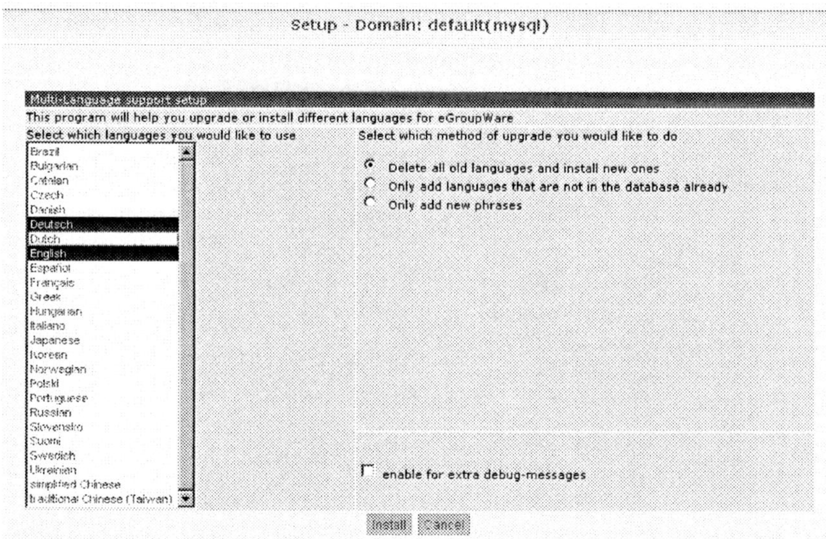

The selection of the languages.

With the language management you can also customize the system charset. To do so, you click on *Current system-charset is not set, click here to change it.* The form *Change system-charset* allows changing the charset. As a general rule this step is not necessary.

Step 5 finally serves the enhanced application management. A large form itemizes the applications. This includes e.g. the application name, its appropriate title, the version and the status information. Here you can also delete applications. If any problem occurs with an application, this will also be indicated by a red cross.

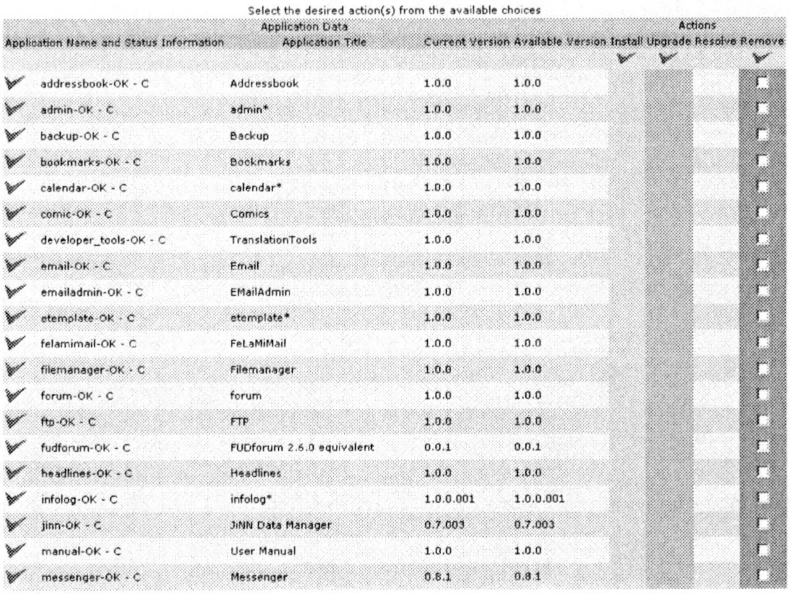
Select the desired action(s) from the available choices

Application Name and Status Information	Application Title	Current Version	Available Version	Install	Upgrade	Resolve	Remove
addressbook-OK - C	Addressbook	1.0.0	1.0.0				
admin-OK - C	admin*	1.0.0	1.0.0				
backup-OK - C	Backup	1.0.0	1.0.0				
bookmarks-OK - C	Bookmarks	1.0.0	1.0.0				
calendar-OK - C	calendar*	1.0.0	1.0.0				
comic-OK - C	Comics	1.0.0	1.0.0				
developer_tools-OK - C	TranslationTools	1.0.0	1.0.0				
email-OK - C	Email	1.0.0	1.0.0				
emailadmin-OK - C	EMailAdmin	1.0.0	1.0.0				
etemplate-OK - C	etemplate*	1.0.0	1.0.0				
felamimail-OK - C	FeLaMiMail	1.0.0	1.0.0				
filemanager-OK - C	Filemanager	1.0.0	1.0.0				
forum-OK - C	forum	1.0.0	1.0.0				
ftp-OK - C	FTP	1.0.0	1.0.0				
fudforum-OK - C	FUDforum 2.6.0 equivalent	0.0.1	0.0.1				
headlines-OK - C	Headlines	1.0.0	1.0.0				
infolog-OK - C	infolog*	1.0.0.001	1.0.0.001				
jinn-OK - C	JiNN Data Manager	0.7.003	0.7.003				
manual-OK - C	User Manual	1.0.0	1.0.0				
messenger-OK - C	Messenger	0.8.1	0.8.1				

With the setup all the installed applications including their status information can be retrieved.

If you choose the *Header Admin Login* in the setup dialogue, you get to a form that the attentive administrator is already acquainted with. It has the title *Setup* and offers apart from a system analysis different preferences (which are already described in chapter 1).

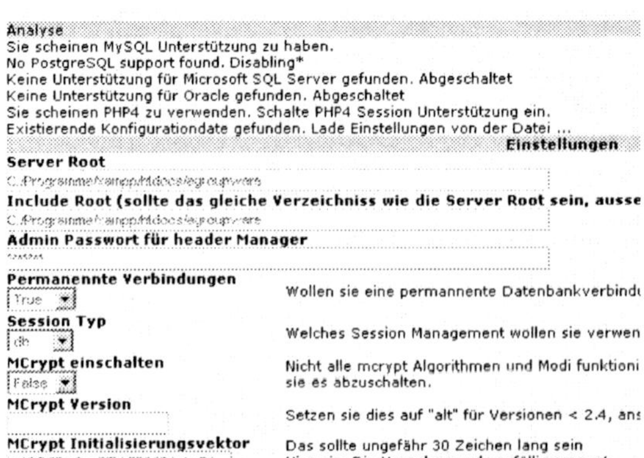

Accessing the eGroupWare preferences.

2.21 User Preferences

Beside the common system settings also each user (and of course each administrator) can customize his environment according to his preferences. To do this, you use the link *Preferences* of the main menu. This function is available for all users. There are only differences between handling the available settings. With these preferences you e.g. define the number of icons in the navigation bar, user shell and theme selection as well as different formats.

The following image shows the preferences of the administrator. Each user is provided the same preferences for his environment. The only difference between the preferences of the administrators and the „normal" users: The administrator is provided the three tabs *Your Preferences*, *Default preferences* and *Forced Preferences* to define not only his own configuration but also the defaults for other users.

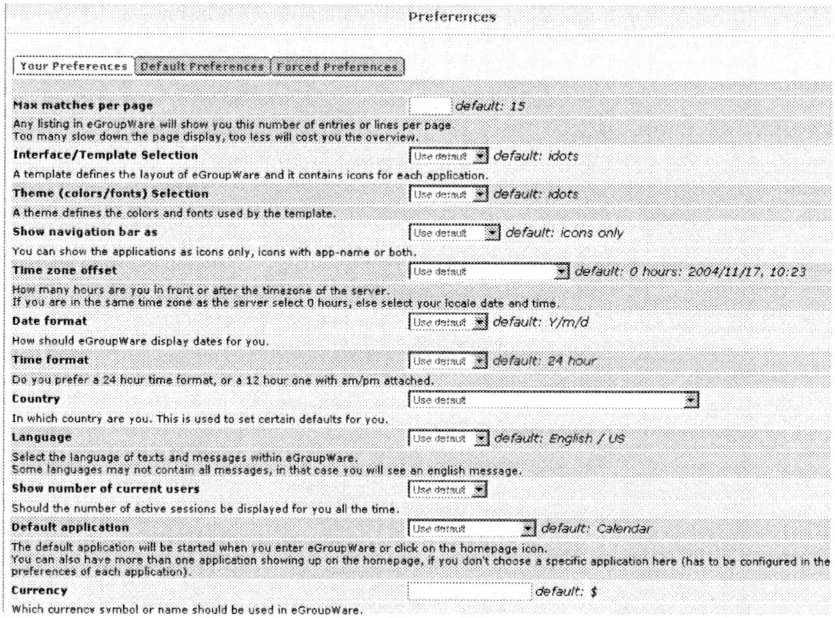

The common preferences of the eGroupWare system.

Let's have a look at the different preferences in their order:

- **Max matches per page:** Each list in eGroupWare displays this number of lines per page. Please note that too many lines slow down the composition of the page. On the other hand the overview lacks if there are not enough. The default is *15*. You should play a little around a little until you have found the ideal number for your own environment.
- **Interface/Template Selection**: With this select menu you define the layout of the interface. The templates define the layout and also the icons it contains. The default is *idots*. There are some more available:

default, *idsociety*, *justweb*, *linux-at-work.de*, *literati* and *verdilak*. Which one you choose is firstly a matter of your taste. We keep to the defaults. This has a certain reason, as we will see below.

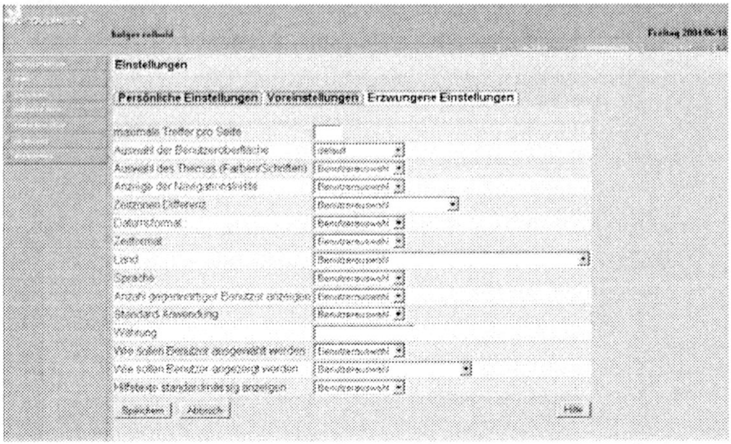

The interface *default* comes along with a very modern design.

- **Theme (colors/fonts) Selection**: The theme definese the colors and fonts of the interface. With the select menu a lot of themes are available. The default here is *idots*.
- **Show navigation bar as**: With this select menu you define whether the applications should be shown as symbol (icon), text or both of them. The default is *icons only*. For the beginning it might be useful to activate *Icons and text* until you know the icons and their appropriate functions.
- **Time zone offset**: Here you define the time zone offset. The default is *0 hours: date and time*. The correct setting depends on the question, how many hours you are in front of the time zone of the server. If you are in the same time zone as the server, you should select 0 hours.
- **Date format**: eGroupWare supports different date formats. Here you define the desired format. The default is *y/m/d*.
- **Time format**: Here you determine whether you prefer a 24 hour time format or the 12 hour format with am/pm attached. By default, eGroupWare uses the 24 hour format.
- **Country**: Here you define in which country you live. Different settings are made.
- **Language**: With the language selection you chose the language of the texts and messages within the eGroupWare environment. The default in our case is *English / US*. Please note that some languages do not provide all the texts. In this case the English text will be displayed.
- **Default application**: With this setting you define the application that should be started if you restart eGroupWare or if you click on the icon of the home page. You can also display several applications. To do this, you do not select an application. Which application will be displayed

then must be configured in the preferences of the according application. The dafault is *Calendar*.

- **Currency**: With this input field you decide which currency symbol or which name eGroupWare should use. The default setting is *$* (Dollar).
- **How would you like to select accounts**: With this setting you define whether the select box shows all available users or whether a new popup window should be opened, in which you can search for the names or groups. The default *Selectbox* may install very slow with many users.
- **How would you like to display accounts**: Here you determine the display of the account names (e.g. *Firstname, Lastname, Username*). For security reasons the user name should not be displayed public.
- **Show help messages by default**: Here you select whether the help messages should be always displayed. The display is activated by default.

If you use the template *idots*, there are further configuration options available:

- **Max number of icons in navigation bar**: With this field you decide how many icons should be shown in the navigation bar at the top of the page. Additional icons will be available in a pulldown menu that can be called by an icon on the far right side of the navigation bar.
- **Autohide Sidebox menu's**: The left navigation menu can be hidden with this switch. By default the menu is activated.
- **Click or Mouse Over to show menus**: Here you define whether you should use a mouse click or a mouse over effect to display the menu.
- **Disable slider effects**: With this switch you can disable the animated slider effects when showing or hiding the navigation menu in the page. Opera and Konquerer users must disable this funktion.
- **Disable Internet Explorer png-image-bugfix**: Here you define whether bugfix scripts for Internet Explorer 5.5 and above for displaying transparent PNG images should be switched off.
- **Show page generation time**: With this last of the available settings you finally can determine whether the page generation time should be shown on the bottom of the page or not.

With the functions described in this chapter you are able to administrate a basic system and customize it according to the individual preferences. In the next step the client applications have to be prepared for the collaboration with the eGroupWare server – and then to use them.

3. Email with eGroupWare

Today electronic mail is the most important communcation medium in many parts. Mostly it has replaced telephone, facsimile and traditional mail. Contrary to the classical mail where messages are transferred from a client on the local system, by using eGroupWare the digital messages leave on the server. The vital advantage: They can be read, answered and deleted from any machine – as far as the access is available to the eGroupWare server. And: The client operating system does not play a role, because the access is based on the web technology.

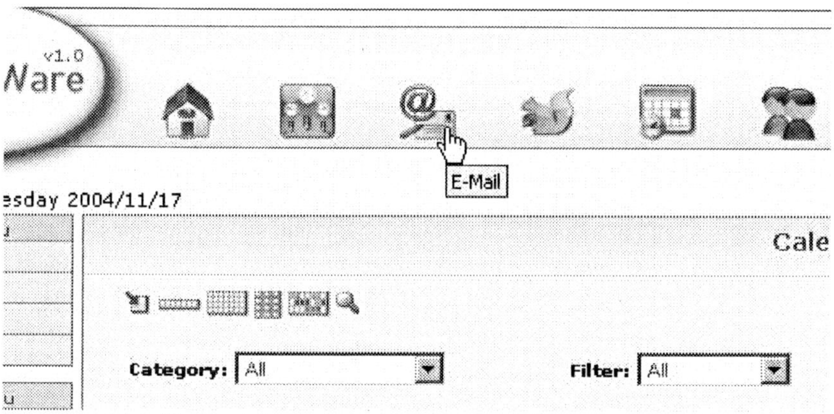

The AngleMail client is accessed by the Email symbol. In this configuration straight next to it you find the FelaMiMail client which has the outline of a bird.

eGroupWare by default comes along with two Email modules: AngleMail (*www.anglemail.org*) and FelaMiMail (*freshmeat.net/projects/felamimail/*). The AngleMail functions are available on the Email symbol in the icon bar, FelaMiMail must – depending on the system and the user configuration – first be activated via the system control. AngleMail is the preconfigured mail application that provides all Email related functions one awaits from a groupware solution. FelaMiMail (*freshmeat.net/projects/felamimail/*) is a IMAP specialist. The web based IMAP client is a brilliant fit in eGroupWare.

The basic requirement to use the Email functions is of course that you have an appropriate mail account on a mail server. eGroupWare is not a messaging system, but plays the role of a web based mail client that gets its mail from a conventional POP3 resp. IMAP server and delivers them over a SMTP server.

Server type and location do not play a role, because the typical messaging functions are based on internet standards. It may also involve a Windows based mail server.

When setting up the messaging functions you should notice one important aspect: user name and password on the mail server and the eGroupWare mail client must be identical. Only this way you can access the server with eGroupWare – and of course also with a traditional mail client auch as e.g. Evolution.

3.1 Utilizing AngleMail

As most of the service prviders and administrators (unfortunately still) set on POP3 for accessing the the post box, we mainly consecrate ourselves to the POP3 specialist AngleMail. If you click on the Email icon for the very first time, eGroupWare presents a dialogue we already faced in chapter 2.15. It is the Email preferences. Here you configure eGroupWare for the collaboration with the POP3/IMAP4 and the SMTP server.

The following settings have to be made:

- Enter your POP/IMAP mail server hostname or IP address
- Select your mail server type
- Enter your default mail domain (From: user@domain)
- Mail server login type
- Enter your SMTP server hostname or IP address
- Enter your SMTP server port
- User for SMTP-authentication (leave it empty if no auth required)
- Password for SMTP-authentication

We will discuss the details later. The messaging functions are configurated in principle. If the information as well as the user ID and the password match the mail server account, you can now retrieve and send your first mails via eGroupWare. After a new click on the Email icon AngleMail presents it's typical interface. Like the other eGroupWare modules also two mail specific menues are available: *mail* and *mail folder*. With the working space you compose new mails, read incoming mails, create filters and edit – if necessary – the mail preferences. With the links *from*, *subject*, *date* and *size* by the way you can sort the mails, too.

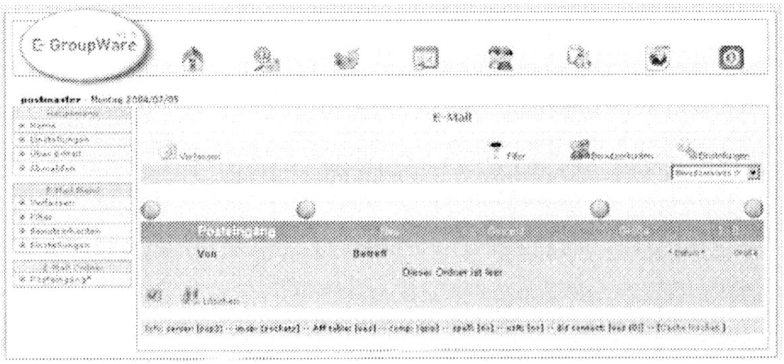

The mail functions are available and ready for use.

Let us have a look at how you master typical tasks like writing and answering mails. Creating is really very simple. To do this, you only click on *New Mail* in the overview. In the appropriate dialogue you fill in the address, CC, BCC, subject and the actual message body. An attachment can optionally be sent on the journey.

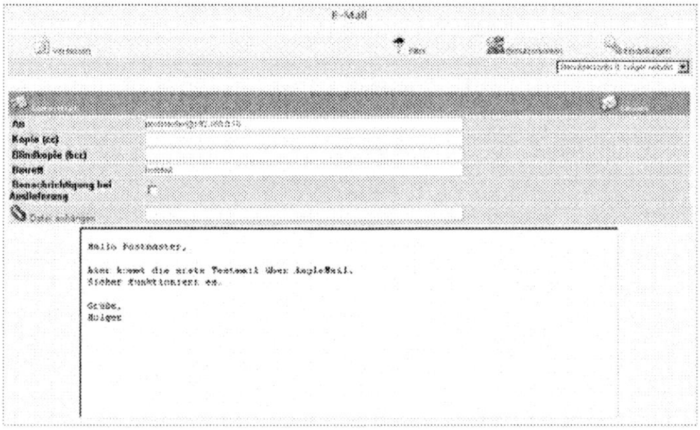

Creating the first mail.

In the email menu you find the link *New mail*, which opens the same dialogue. With the link *Adresbook* a new window opens with which you can access the addressbook. The dispatch is initiated by a simple click on *send.*

Reading of a mail is likewise very easy. If you received new mails, then this is indicated for example on the own homepage with the next login (see following illustration). Clicking on the subject listed here opens the mail.

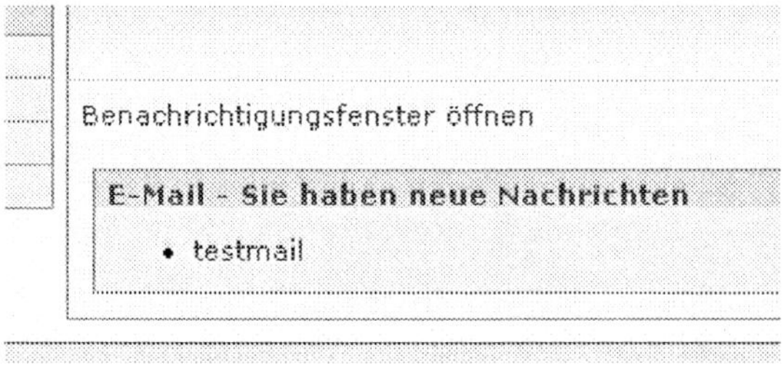

The homepage announces a new message.

Alternatively you open a mail by clicking on the email icon of the tool bar. In the inbox new mails are to be found. Clicking on the subject opens the mail. It shows the typical header fields *from*, *to*, *date* and *subject* as well as, of course, the actual message information.

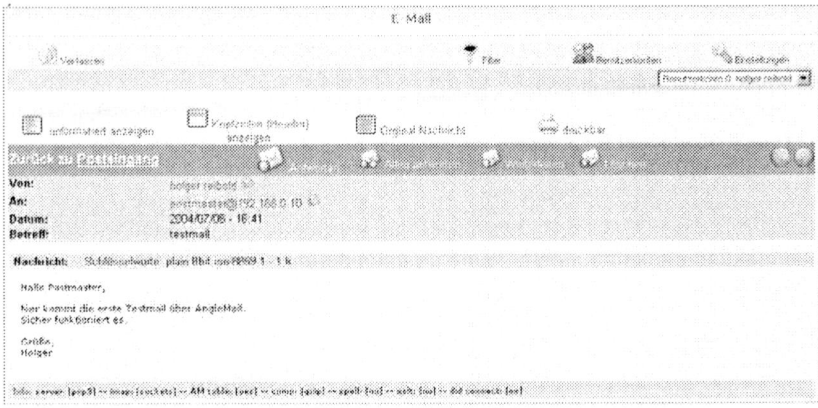

An email opened in inbox.

With the email view alle further important email functions are available, especially

- Show unformatted
- Show header
- printable
- Reply
- Peply all
- Forward
- Delete

The most important function is most probably that for replying a mail. To do this, you simply click on *Reply*. The addressee, subject and quoted mail will already be inserted in the reply form that opens. The answering must only fill in its text and initiate the mail.

The inbox still has another useful function to offer: Beside the sender and the addressee of an email you find a small icon, which symbolizes a vcard. If you click on it, then the person can be added to the addressbook. The dialogue shown in the following illustration opens, with which you can edit, copy and, with *finish*, store in the addressbook. Beside the entry can be added into the InfoLog module for the further task management.

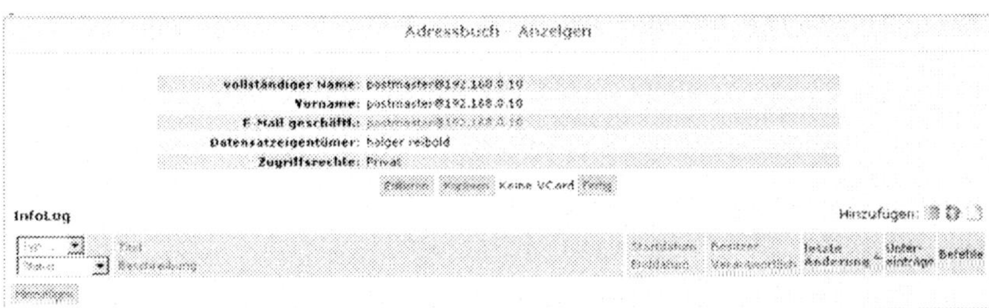

The contact information of a mail sender land in the addressbook.

In the upper area of the mail overview you find another three useful functions, which are also available via the email menu:

- filter
- accounts
- settings

As with the link *filter* you access the filter settings resp. create new filters, you can access the mail accounts set up for a user and create new accounts with *accounts*. If you create a new user, then you likewise get to the email preferences, which will be describes in detail in the following section.

With the filter preferences you specify how to proceed with mails which match a certain criteria. In doing so, you can combine different operators. Besides, with the filter dialogue it is possible to test the filter settings. After you have saved the filter with *Send*, it will be displayed in the filter list and can be edited there if necessary.

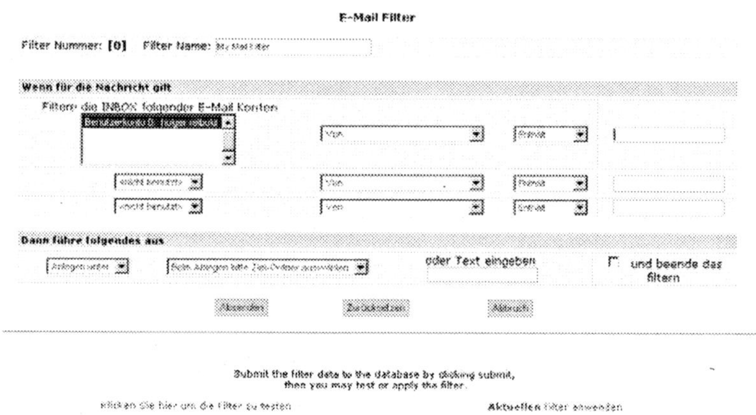

Adding a new filter.

3.2 Email preferences

With the Email preferences users can customize their environment according to their needs. If you create a new user account, you get to the same document. There are two differences: In the first case the form has the title *Standard Email prefercences*, when creating a new account, the form is named *Email Extra Account *** Number x*, whereas x starts with the number one. When creating a new account the option *Enable this email account* is additionally available.

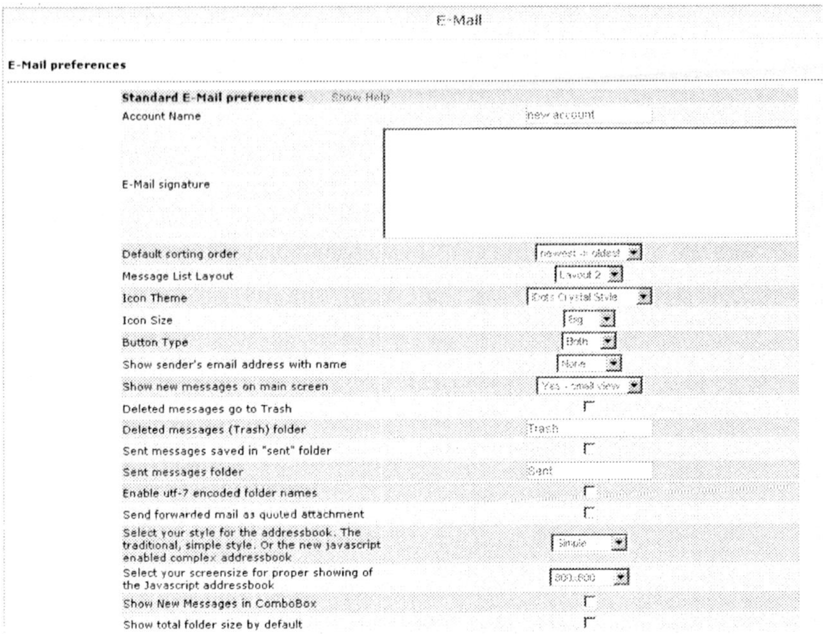

The form for creating a new user account.

The options in detail:

- **Enable this email account**: This option is only available, if there has already been an account created for the user. You activate this option, if the second or further accounts should also be used beside standard account.
- **Account Name**: Here you insert the name that should be displayed for the email accounts in the select box. If you do not insert anything, the account will be assigned a standard name, e.g. *account[0]: name.* Thereby first name and last name are the complete name of the eGroupWare account. If you want to use a specific name you fill it in here. Important: The account name given here only serves for the identfication of the user account. For emails sent the name will be used as dispatcher which has been indcated as email address.
- **Email signature**: Here you insert the so called signature, which means the text which for this email account will be added at the bottom of the mail. You should notice that AngleMail does not support HTML tags yet. By the way, there will not be a signature added to forwarded emails.
- **Default sorting order**: Here you determine how the sorting should happen on the mail view. By default the mails are sorted by date, author, size or subject. Instead of the default setting *newest -> oldest* the sorting can also be inverted.
- **Message List Layout**: Here you can choose between two layouts for the mail index page.

- **Icon Theme**: AngleMail supports the usage of different groups of icons. The actual available icons are based on Evolution and the Mozilla browser. With the select menu there are another three available: *Noia @Carlius Style*, *Aqua Fusion* and *iDots Crystal Style*.
- **Icon Size**: With this select menu you can determine the different sizes of the icons. Thereby you can choose between big and small.
- **Button Type**: eGroupWare provides different kinds of buttons. They can be displayed as text, images or text and image.
- **Show sender's email addresse with name**: The function of this option is misunderstood sometimes. If you open a folder with emails, *From* can display three pieces of information:
    - The name of the sender, if given at all.
    - Email address plus name.
    - The reply Email address of the sender, if this differs from the from address.

  Mostly users set this selection on *No*. This means that only the name of the sender will be displayed. If there was no name delivered by the sender, the from address will be displayed. Also if a separate reply to address has been delivered, this has no influnce on it, because the from address will always be used, if no name is available.
- **Show new messages on main screen:** Here you determine, which information should be displayed on the overview page of a user. The default setting displays a short amount of the messages in the inbox (of the standard mail account). Alternatively the options *Yes* and *No* are available.

Deleted messages go to Trash: If you activate this option, deleted messages land in the eGroupWare trash bin. The name of the folder can be defined with the field *Folder for deleted mails (trash)*. But this function is only available for IMAP servers, because POP servers do not own such a folder.

- **Deleted messages (Trash) folder**: see above.
- **Sent messages saved in "sent" folder**: This function is only available when using an IMAP server. Here you activate storing of sent mails in the *sent* folder.
- **Sent messages folder**: Here you define the IMAP folder for sent mails.
- **Enable utf-7 encoded folder names**: You activate this option if folder names should contain Non-US-ASCII characters. Also this function is only available for an IMAP server. Normaly it will not be needed and can therefore remain deactivated.
- **Send forwarded mail as quoted attachment**: If forwarded mails should be tied to the mail as attachments, you activate this option.
- **Select your style for the addressbook. The traditional, simple style. Or the new javascript enabled complex addressbook**: There are two kinds of addressbooks available: the simple and the complexe variant. The complexe variant suits for bigger organizations.
- **Select your screensize for proper showing of the Javascript addressbook**: Here you define the size of the JavaScript addressbook. There are three sizes selectable: 800x600, 1024x768 und 1200x1600 pixels.

- **Show number of messages in Folder**: If the amount of new messages should be displayed in the folder view, you activate this option.
- **Show total folder size by default**: Also the whole size of the folder can be displayed in the standard view. If this is desired, you activate this option.

Following are the user defined preferences:

- **Use custim settings:** Here you activate the usage of the user defined preferences.
- **Email Account Name**: Here you fill in the name of the account.
- **Email password (hidden)**: Here you insert the password that is required for his email account.
- **Email address**: In this input filed you insert the address that should be used in the field *from*.
- **Mail Server**: Here you define the name of the email server you draw your mails from.
- **Mail Server type**: Here you determine the mail server type. There are POP3 and IMAP as well as the secured versions available.
- **IMAP Server Type – If Applicable**: If you use an IMAP server, you can here define the kind of the IMAP server. By default the option *Cyrus* or *Courier* is provided. Alternatively there are UWash and UW-Maildir possible. In case of doubt you should consult the mail server administrator.
- **U-Wash Mail Folder – If Applicable**: This option is necessary if you use the UWash IMAP server.

Client binding

When accessing eGroupWare you are by no means limited to using a browser. Up to now there exists a so called connector for the Personal Information Manager Contact (*kontact.org*). It allows binding KDE clients to the eGroupWare solution. The binding is made by the command *egroupwarewizard*. It takes delivery of the relevan data as server name, user name and password.

There is also a connector in development for the Microsoft Outlook client. You may be assured that further binding modules will follow, e.g. for Evolution.

3.3 FelaMiMail

The web based mail client FelaMiMail has a lot of interesting functions. It allows reading and replying of mails, which the system obtains from an IMAP server. This client very clearly shows the advantages of IMAP: You can create arbitrary folders, sort new incoming mail in certain deposits at once etc. – everything you are acquainted with from your graphical mail client, but just on server side. In order to use the IMAP client you need an account on an IMAP server of course.

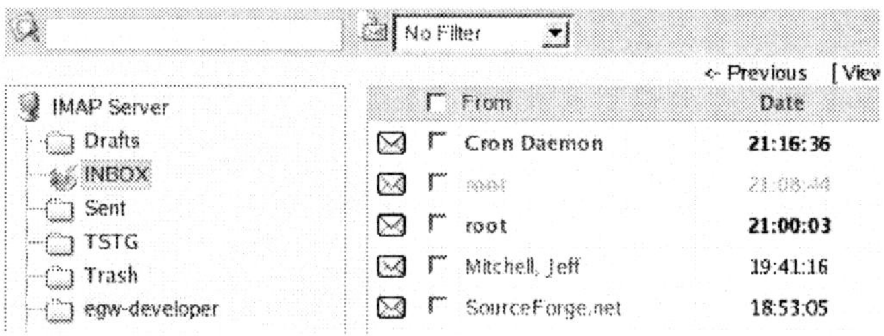

A glance at the web based mail client FelaMiMail.

Also FelaMiMail has a menu of its own with which you create and send mails. With the FelaMiMail preferences you can customize different settings of the module and manage folders.

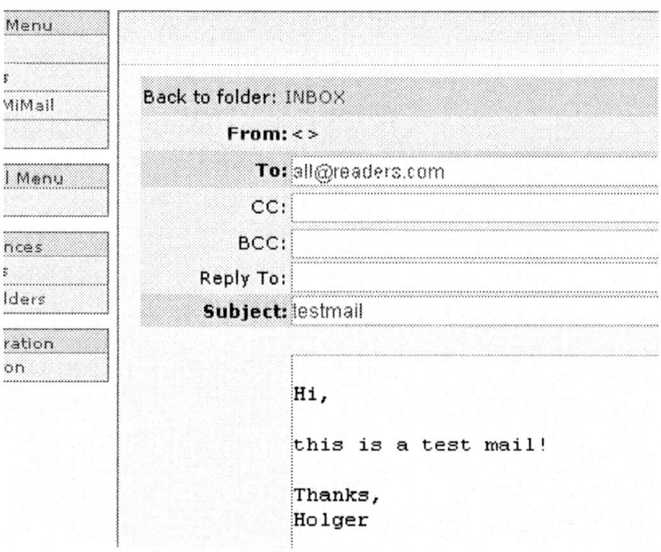

A message arises in the FelaMiMail client.

4. Appointment management

The second important component of the eGroupWare system is, the calendar function. It primarily acts as an appointment and task management system. Both areas are overlapping naturally. After logging in, eGroupWare by default presents the calendar view with its typical elements. Beneath the tool bar you find the calendar function, which opens the day view. Next follows another small tool bar, with which you activate the views *Today, This Week, This Month, This Year, Planner* and *Daily Matrix View.* The same functions are available with the calender menu in the left window area.

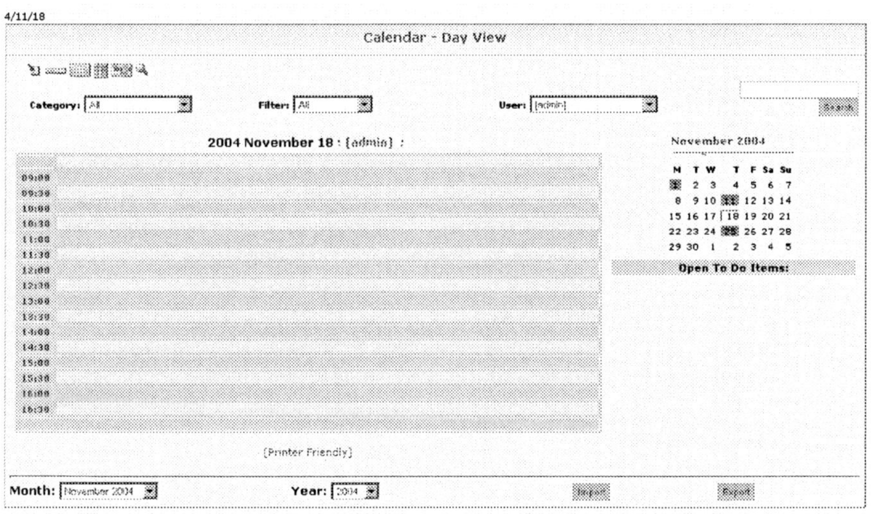

The typical calendar view of eGroupWare.

Beneath the view bar there are three select menues from which you choose the view of the categories, filters and users. Besides, a search function is available, which helps you trawl the systeme.

Next follows the view of the current date including the current user as well the actual day view. The day view displays a temporal division in half hour measure. With a standard installation, aside the overview a monthly view as well as a listing of outstanding tasks will be shown. Finally you can edit the current month and year view at the bottom of the page. Also, the import function for iCalender resp. vCalender based data is available here.

The day view lists the arising appointments including a short description and further detailed information. E.g. an orange dot characterizes a single appointment. Repetetive appointments are indicated by a double arrow. In the day view you can also recognize whether an appointment is assigned to one person or to several. An appointment in which several users take part is indicated by multiple person's icons. If you move the mouse cursor over the appointment entry, you can access detail information such as the names of the participants in the info window.

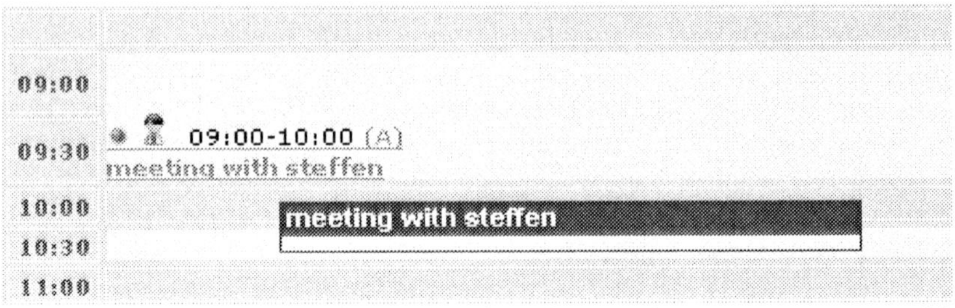

With the day view detail information fort the appointments are accessable.

4.1 Creating and editing a calendar entry

Creating a new calendar entry is rather easy. To do this, you click in the calender menu on the link *New Entry* or you click on the desired date in the day view. In the week view you click at the appropriate day on the plus sign. It always opens the dialogue *Calendar Add.* It first receives the title of the entry and then a description. Next follows the choice of the category – if there have been created any at all.

With the following select fields you determine the location, the start date, the start time, the end date, the end time and the priority. If it is a private appointment, you activate the according option.

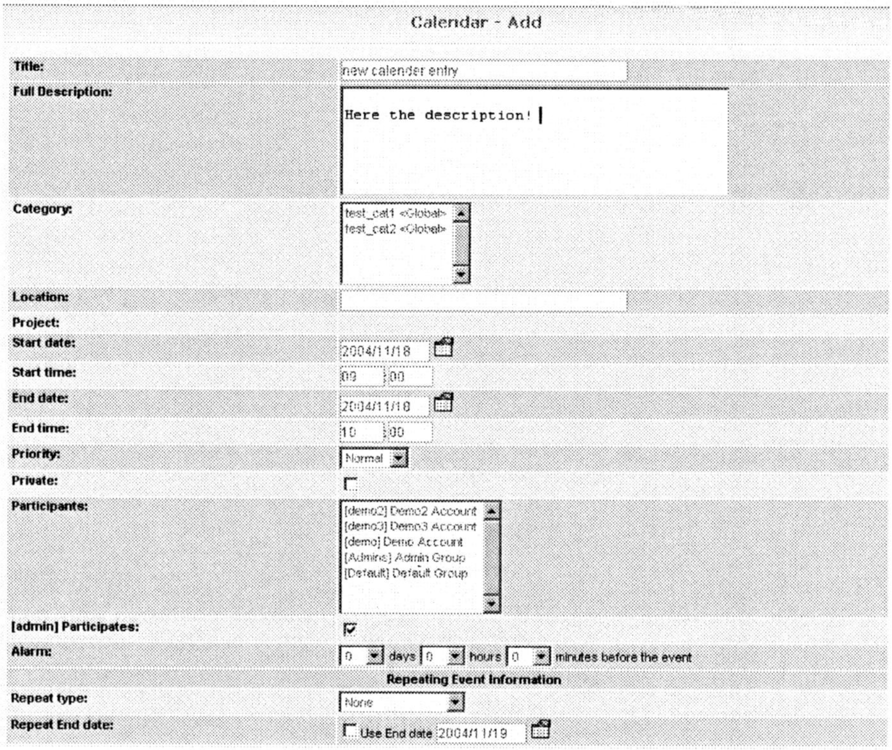

A new calendar entry arises.

With the following select menu you choose further participants. If the participant that sets the appointment participates too, the option *user name participates* must be activated. Next follow the settings for the alarms. Here you determine how many days, hours and minutes before the event alarms should be given out.

The ending of the form for creating a new date is made by the preferences for repeating events. Hereby you first determine the repeat type (*daily, weekly, monthly – by day, monthly – by date, yearly*). Besides you can define an end time for the repeat date. If it is a weekly repeated day, you can determine the day explicitly. The form also provides an interval repeation. After a click on *Save* the new calendar entry will be added into the day view.

To edit an entry you just click on it in the overview. eGroupWare opens an overview with the following information:

- Title
- Description
- Location
- Start Date/Time
- End Date/Time
- Priority
- Access
- Participants

- Created by
- Updated
- Repetition

To make changes for a calendar entry, you click on *Edit*. By doing this you open the dialogue described above for creating a calendar entry. With the overview there are another two useful functions available: With *Alarm Management* the alarm functions will be faded in, with *Export* the date can be exported. Also the deletion of an entry with the according button is possible here. Thereby a security query will occur whether the date should be really deleted or not.

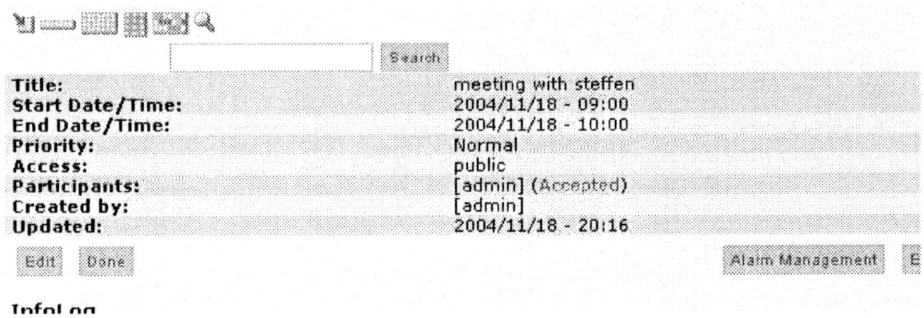

The summarization of a calendar entry.

In the date summary you also find the functions for accepting or rejecting an appointment. Behind each designated participant you find a link as e.g. in the illustration above the link *Accepted.* A click opens the dialogue *Change Status*. Here you can accept or reject the appointment or even agree provisionally (*tentative*). In the calendar view acceptions, rejections and tentative offers are indicated by the characters *A, R* and *T* behind the user name.

With the appointment summary you can accept or even reject appointments.

4.2 Calendar preferences

With the calendar menu the calendar preferences are available, with which you can use a variety of configuration possibilities. The settings in sequence:

- **Default calendar view**: Here you determine which of the possible views should be displayed as default when the calendar will be opened. The default is *Daily*. The other options are *Weekly, Monthly, Yearly, Planner by category* and *Planner by user, a*s already mentioned above.
- **Show default view on main screen**: Here you define the standard view of the eGroupWare start page. This page opens when you log in. The default is *No*. Alternative preference is *Yes*.
- **Receive email updates**: Do you want to be notified about new or changed appointments? If yes, activate the notification with this switch. Interesting thereby: You can limit the notifications on certain changes. Each line includes the notifications of all the above listed. All modifications include the title, description, participants, but no responses of the participants. If the creator of an event requests a response, he too automatically recieves the responses of the participants, as acceptions and rejections. The default is *Never*. Other preferences are:
    - *on invitation / cancelation only*
    - *on time change of more than 4 hours too*
    - *on any time change too*
    - *on all modification, but responses*
    - *on participant responses too*

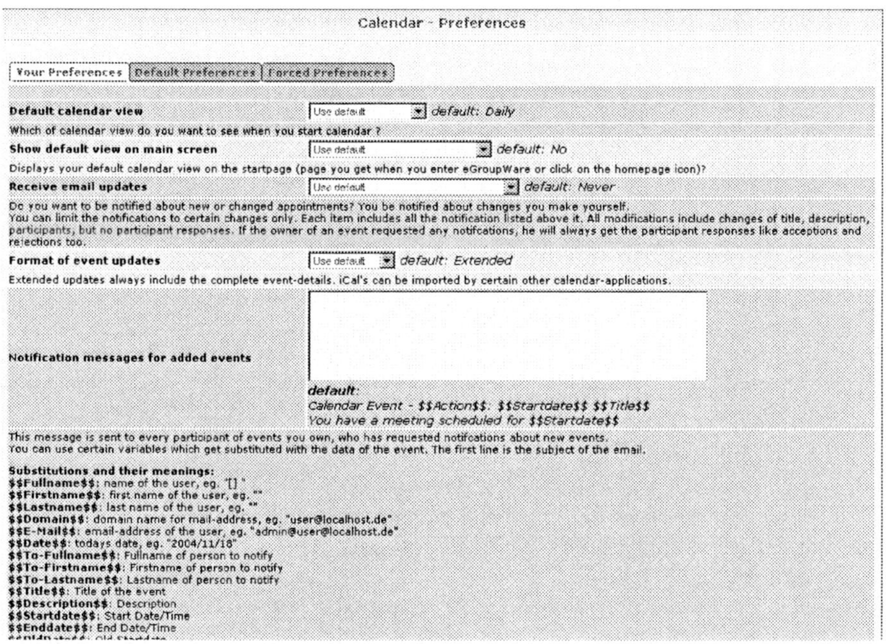

With the menu *Calendar – Preferences* the calendar view can be customized to the individual needs.

- **Format of event updates**: With this field you edit the extended updates. Thereby iCalendar entries of other calendar programs can be imported. The default is *Extended.* Alternative preferences are:
    - *None*

- *iCa l / rfc2445*

- **Notification messages for added events**: The message deposited here will be sent to all participants of the appointment, who want the notification. Thereby it is possible to use certain variables that are replaced by the data of the event. The first line is the subject of the email. The default is:
  Calendar Event - $$Action$$: $$Startdate$$ $$Title$$
  You have a meeting scheduled for $$Startdate$$.
  The explanation of the replacements and their meanings:
  - *$$*Fullname*$$:*: name of the user, e.g. *holger reibold.*
  - $$Firstname$$: first name of the user, e.g. *holger.*
  - $$Lastname$$: last name of the user, eg. *reibold.*
  - $$Domain$$: domain name for mail address, e.g. *7eleven.de.*
  - $$Email$$: email address of the user, e.g. *admin@7eleven.de.*
  - $$Date$$: currenmt date, e.g. 2004/06/20.
  - $$To-Fullname$$: Fullname of person to notify.
  - $$To-Firstname$$: Firstname of person to notify.
  - $$To-Lastname$$: Lastname of person to notify.
  - $$Title$$: Title of the event
  - $$Description$$: Description
  - $$Startdate$$: Start Date/Time
  - $$Enddate$$: End Date/Time
  - $$OldDate$$: Old Startdate
  - $$Category$$: Category
  - $$Location$$: Location
  - $$Priority$$: Priority
  - $$Participants$$: Participants
  - $$Owner$$: Owner
  - $$Repetition$$: Repetition details (or empty)
  - $$Action$$: Action that caused the notification: Added, Cancelled, Accepted, Rejected.
  - $$Link$$: Link to view the event.

- **Notification messages for cancelled events**: The message defined here will be sent for rejeceted or cancelled events. The default is:
  Calendar Event - $$Action$$: $$Startdate$$ $$Title$$
  Your meeting scheduled for $$Startdate$$ has been canceled.
- **Notification messages for modified events**: This message will be sent for modified events. The default is:
  Calendar Event - $$Action$$: $$Startdate$$ $$Title$$
  Your meeting that had been scheduled for $$OldDate$$ has been rescheduled to $$Startdate$$.
- **Notification messages for your responses**: This message will be sent if you accept, tentatively accept, or reject an event. The default:
  Calendar Event – $$Action$$: $$Startdate$$ $$Title$$
  On 2004/10/18 holger reibold $$Action$$ your meeting request for $$Startdate$$

- **Notification messages for your alarms**: This message will be sent when you set an alarm for a specific event. Also here the default preferences can be enhanced by further information. The default is:
  Alarm for $$Title$$ at $$Startdate$$ in $$Location$$
  Here is your requested alarm.
- **Show invitations you rejected**: Here you define which invitations have been rejected and are still shown in the calendar. Thereby you can accept invitations later on, e.g. after you have solved overlapping events. The default is *No*. The only further option: *Yes*.
- **Display Status of Events**: With this select menu you determine the status (Accepted, Rejected, etc.) of the participants that will be shown in brackets after each participant's name. The default is *Yes*. Alternatively you can hide the status with *No*.
- **Weekday starts on**: Here you define the day which should be shown as first day in the week or month view. The default setting is *Monday*. Alternatively you can select *Sunday* or *Saturday*.
- **Work day starts on**: With this function you define the start of the working day in the day view. All events before this time are shown above. The default: *9:00*.
- **Work day ends**: With this preference you define the end of the working day in the day view. All entries after this time will be shown below. The default is *17:00*.
- **Intervals in day view**: This preference determines the time scale in minutes of the calendar day view. The default: *30*.
- **default appointment length (in minutes)**: Herewith you determine the default for the length of new calendar entries. The length will be displayed in minutes, e.g. with the default *60* (for 1 hour).
- **Preselected group for entering the planner**: Here you determine the group as default that should be shown when the planner is opened. With the select menu the already created groups are available.
- **Intervals per day in planner view**: Here you define the number of time intervals that should be shown in the planner. The default: *4*.
- **Default calendar filter**: With this menu you define which events should be shown if the calendar is opened. The default is *All*. Alternatively *Private Only* can be used.
- **Set new events to private**: If an account is used mostly or only for private purposes, you should create the new event as privat in general. To do this, this option must be set on *Yes*. The default nevertheless is *No*.
- **Print the mini calendars**: In the calendar view by default you find the so called mini calendar. With this switch its view can be activated resp. deactivated. By default it is activated.
- **Print calendars in black & white**: With this last switch finally you can activate the printer friendly view in black and white.

With the preferences menu there are another two functions available: *Grant Access* and *Edit Categories*. With the form *Grant Access* you define the access rights for the groups and users. With the function *Edit Categories* you can edit existing categories or create new ones.

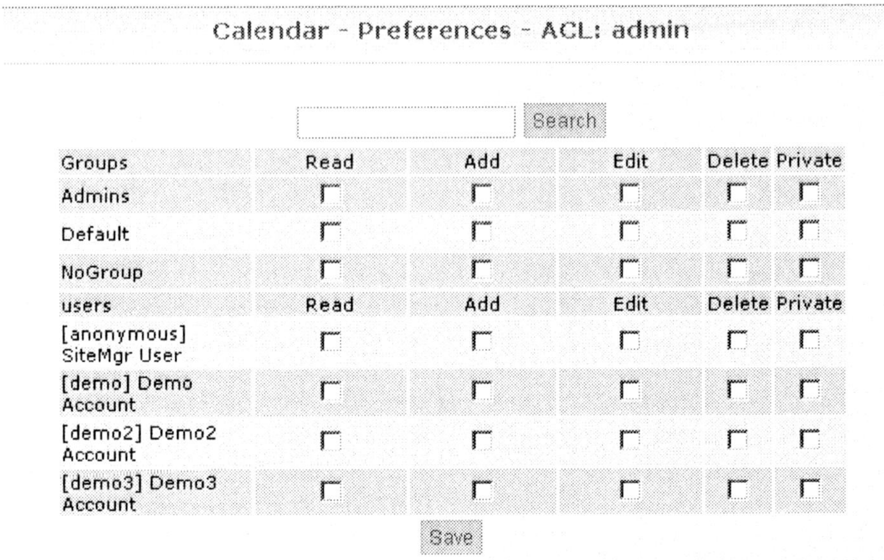

The preferences for the access control on calendar information.

5. Managing contacts

Contacts and addresses are generally an important good for enterprises. As it is right and proper for a professional environment, eGroupWare also disposes of an efficient address and contact management. The according functions are available with the icon *Addressbook* of the tool bar. Here you create new entries, edit the addressbook view, import and export data. Also the common use of this database is possible.

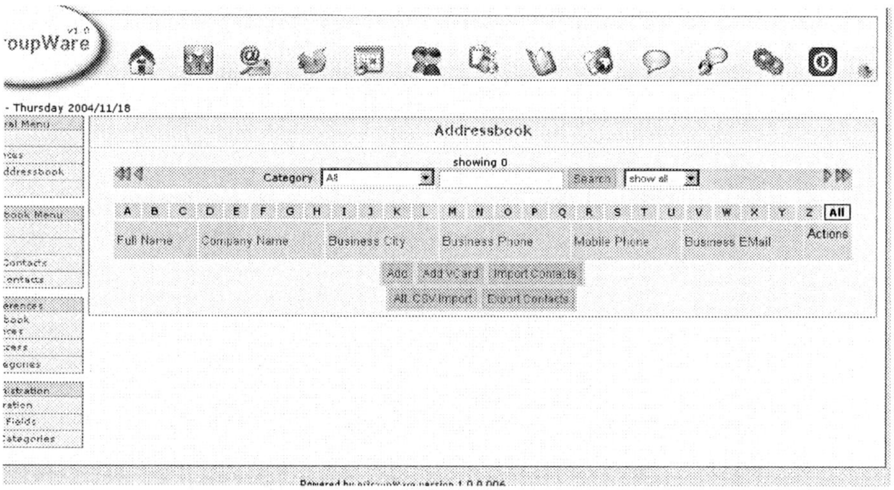

The addressbook view in a rough state.

In rough state eGroupWare presents a simple form which first of all must be filled with data. With the green arrows it allows jumping to and from multilateral addressbooks, provides a select menu for determining the view, a search function as well as different functions for adding, importing and exporting. Above these functions the amount of current entries is indicated. By default for each entry the full name, the company name, the business city, the business phone, the mobile phone and the business email are displayed.

In the left window area under the main menu the most important addressbook functions and the addressbook preferences of the according user are available. With the addressbook preferences e.g. the view of the addressbook entries can be customized.

5.1 Adding an entry

In order to feed the still empty addressbook with information, you click on *Add*. The large form *Addressbook – Add* receives all imaginable information, especially

- personal data like first and last name etc.
- business data like company name, address, public key etc.
- private informationen like address and further private contact information etc.

Finally an address can be marked as privat or associated with an existing category.

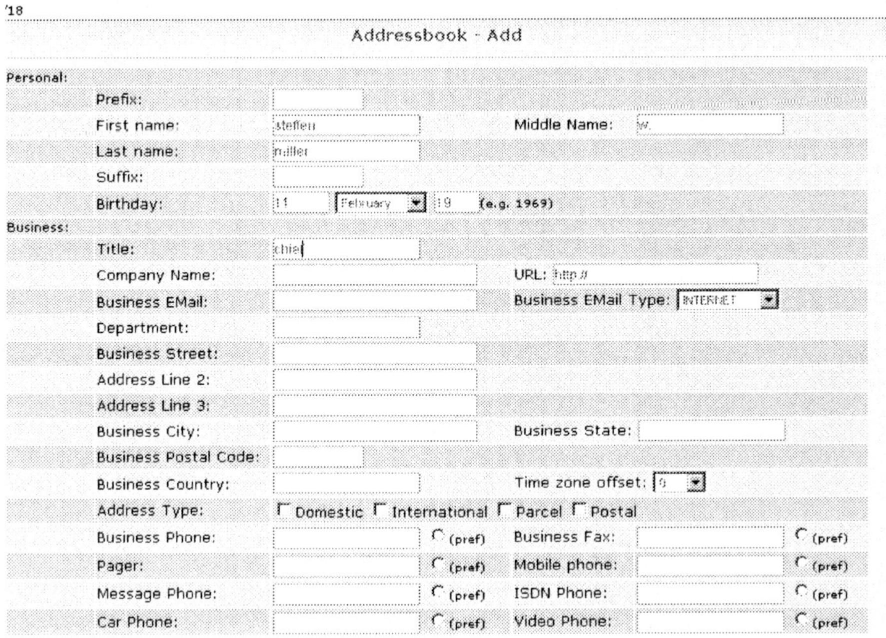

The dialogue for adding an addressbook entry.

With a click on the button *Save* at the bottom of the form you save the input. eGroupWare presents an overview with the form entries. With *Done* you close the process. Besides the entry can be edited, saved as vCard and copied.

If you finally confirm creating the new entry you get back to the addressbook view, where now the newly created contact can be found. You can now display, edit, and delete it with the command column. If the addressbook has several entries and you want to delete them, just activate the according checkbox and click on *Delete* beneath.

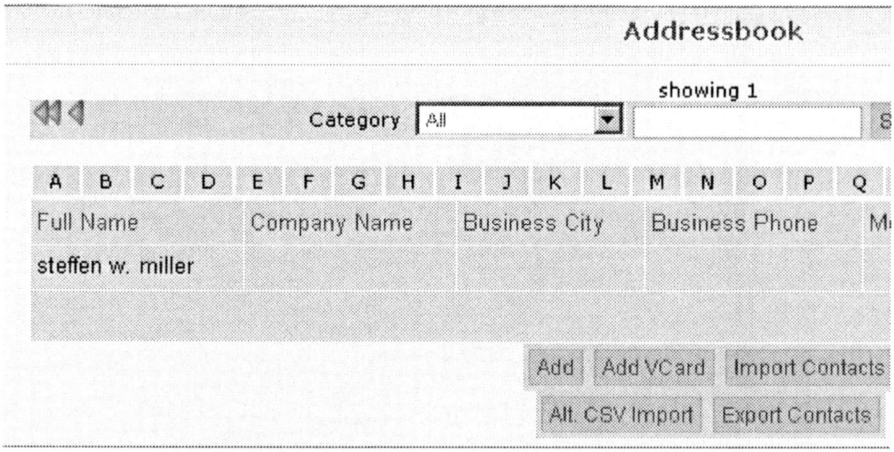

The addressbook has a first entry.

5.2 Importing and exporting contacts

The eGroupWare addressbook supports several import and export functions. E.g. the environment can import especally LDIF-, vCard and CSV based data. Besides the export in several targets formats are possible.

Importing VCards is very easy. To do so, you simply click on *Add VCard.* In the according form you browse to the digital VCard and click on *Load Vcard.*

The import function is more flexible. It allows importing LDIF, CSV and VCard. It even assists in how to prepare existing contacts of the Netscape browser, of MS Outlook or a PalmPilots for the import. In the first input field you enter the path of the file to import. In the following select field you determine the source format. The following options are available:

- Import multiple VCard
- Import from Mozilla
- Import from Netscape
- Import from Outlook - Deutsch
- Import from Outlook - English
- Import from Outlook - Espanol
- Import from Outlook - French
- Import from Outlook - Italiano

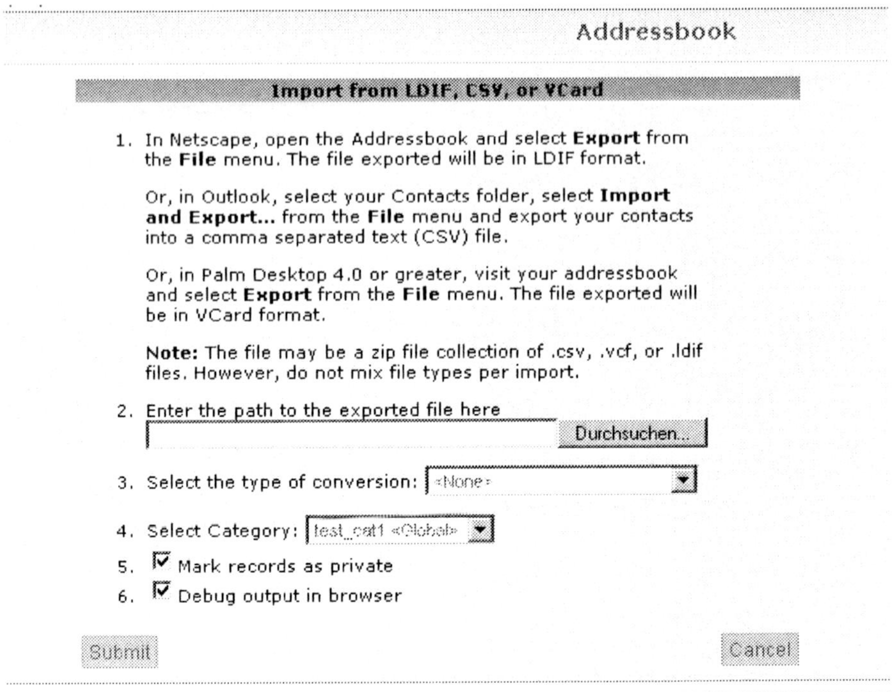

The eGroupWare addressbook supports the import of different contact formats.

Finally you select a category and mark the new entry as privat. Besides the debug output can be shown in the browser. You can watch the current conversion and possible problems. The import process is ended by a click on *Submit*. If no problems have occurred, the system displays the successful import of different entries.

The third import function is available with the button *Alt. CSV Import*. This function we met above already. Here you select the CSV file, the seperator and the charset used for the file, and finally click on *Import*.

More exiting are the export functions, which you e.g. need for exchanging contacts with others. You open the appropriate form with *Export Contacts*. In the export form you first define the target format. There are nine formats available:

- Mozilla LDIF
- Multiple VCard
- Netscape LDIF
- Outlook CSV - Deutsch
- Outlook CSV - English
- Outlook CSV - Français
- Palm PDB
- phpgw LDIF
- phpgw SQL

Next you name the target file, e.g. *export.txt* and select the category. Then you activate the option *Download Export file* and click on *Submit*. The typical downlowad dialogue of the browser opens in which you determine the target of the export file.

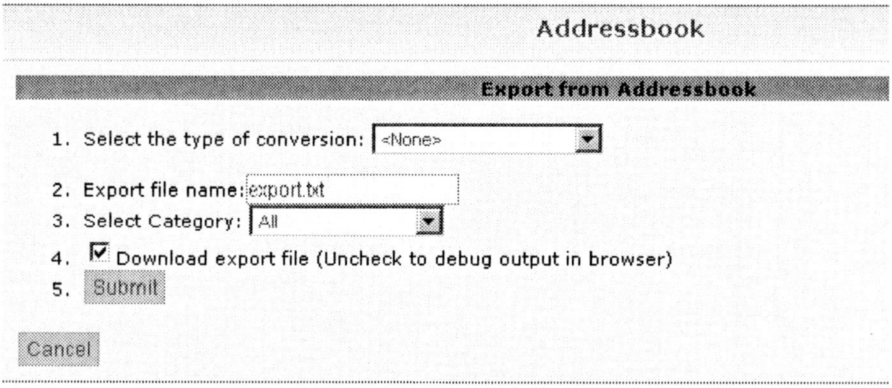

The export function of the eGroupWare adressbook supports nine adress-book formats.

5.3 Addressbook preferences

As already known from other eGroupWare modules, the addressbook preferences can also be edited. To do so, you use the preferences menu on the left window border. A click on *Addressbook preferences* opens the appropriate functions.

Here you find the different contact categories again, which we met at the beginning of the chapter. In the categories *Personal, Business, Home, Extra Phone Numbers* and *Other Fields* the information is activated, which should be displayed in the address list. If there should be further information displayed, just activate the additional fields – or deactivate them, if certain information is not desired.

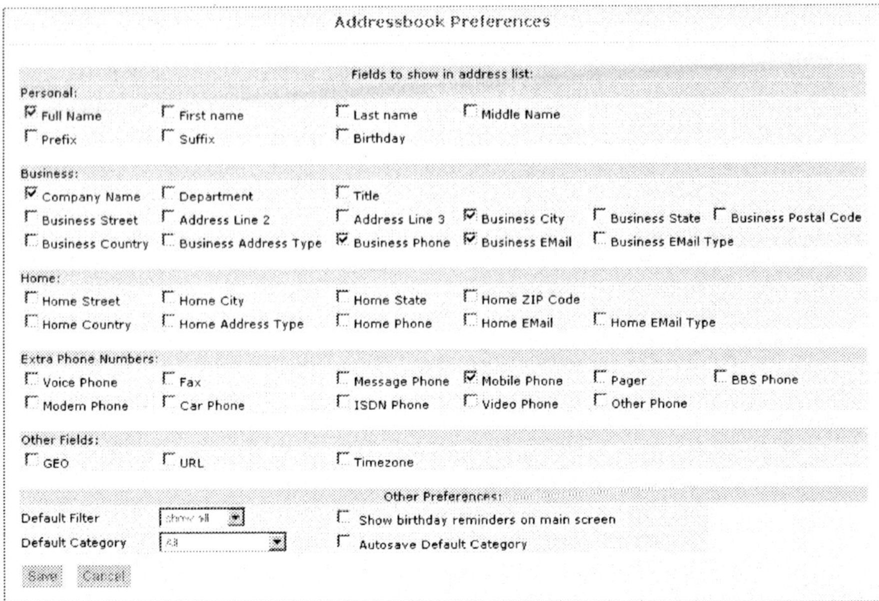

The addressbook preferences.

The only characterstic of this dialogue: The other preferences at the bottom of the form. With the filter, you can limit here the view to all or only private contacts, select the default category and show the so called birthday reminder on the main screen.

6. Project management

The eGroupWare system also provides a flexible and powerful module for the project management. The according functions are installed by default, but not available for the users (and also not for the administrator). They must first be activated by the system administrator via the user resp. the group management. The module developed by Bettina Gille is easy to handle and yet powerful. It supports jobs, accountancy, work hours lists, several statistics and also Access Control Lists.

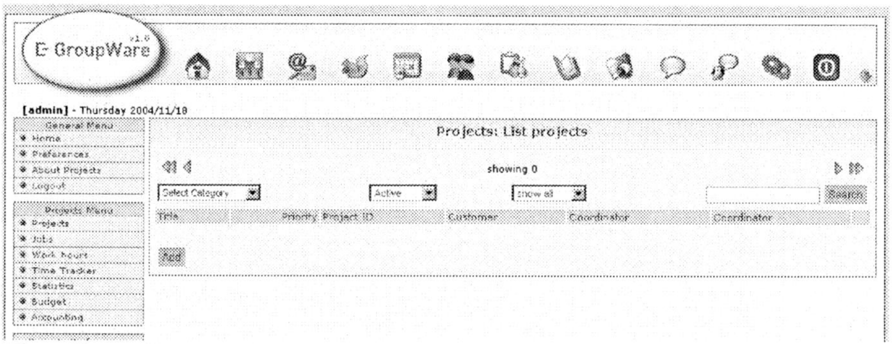

The eGroupWare project management and its specific menues.

In the project view existing projects are itemized including their description and detail information such as project title and ID, coordinator, jobs etc. In the overview, also called project list, you can limit the view to categories and status. There is also a search function available here.

Obvious is that after activating the project function another three menues are to be found below the main menu:

- Projects Menu
- Projects Preferences
- Projects Administration

To create a new project, you click in the project list on the link *Add*. If the country and the currency have not been determined in the system configuration, the header line of the form *Add project* will display the following error message:

```
Error: please specify country and currency in the global preferences section*
```

This problem is solved quickly by editing the system configuration.

In the form you then step by step enter the investment number, the project ID, title, description, previous project, category, customer, coordinator, employees and status. With the option *Generate Project ID* the system creates an ID. Next follow the preferences for the budget and the budget costs for the current month.

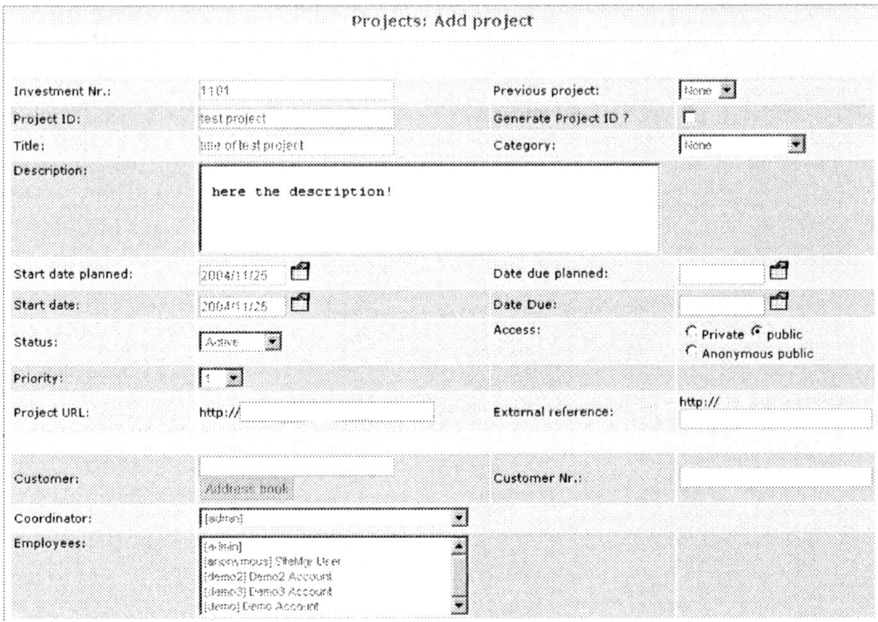

The form for creating a new project.

With the form you can determine the planned time in working hours, the start and due date as well as billable and not billable factors. In the lower dialog area you find the link *Milestones*. With a click on *Save* the newly created project lands in the project list, with which you can edit the entry.

The form for creating milestones is rather simple. It just recieves the title and the planned date of the hop.

If you have created a new project, it is possible to create a job via the link *Jobs* in the project list. To do so, you first click on *Job* and get to the so called jobs list. The link *Add* is available here, too. The according form corresponds to the above described except for small things. The differencies: In the upper form area the main project and the superior project are listed. After saving the job preferences via the button *Save* you get back to the jobs list. Interesting with the jobs: They can be subdivided into jobs.

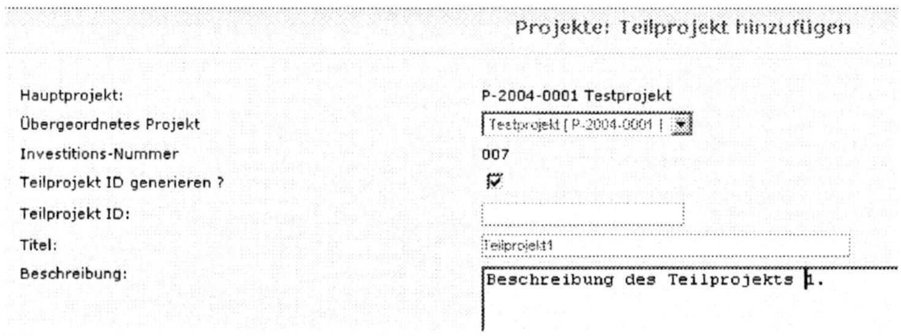

The preferences for a new job.

With the project menu you not only can comfortably access the different projects and jobs , but also call certain statistics. With the link *Work hours* you e.g. can calculate the work hours of each employee including the labour costs thereby incurred. Besides you can have an insight into closed projects in the project archive including typical information (ID, title, coordinator, cistomer, due date, jobs, deliveries, invoices and statistics).

6.1 Project preferences and administration

The project preferences are rather simple. You can define here different notifications, control access and edit the already known categories. If you click on *Preferences* in the menu *Projects Preferences*, you can edit the project preferences of the current project in the according dialogue.

There are four questions:

- Does one want to be informed if a due date of a milestone has changed?
- Does one want to be informed if project data have changed?
- Does one want to be informed if one is assigned to a project?
- Should the project information be shown on the main screen of the user?

To activate the individual functions, mark the check box with a hook and then accept the changes mad by the button *Save*.

With the project preferences you can control access to projects and their preferencies. To do this, you just click on *Grant access* in the menue *Peferencies.*

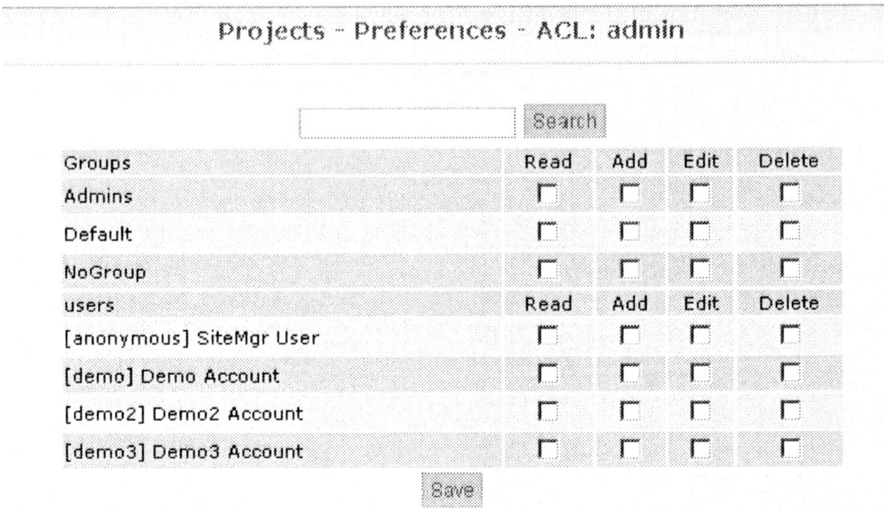

The access control for projects.

The form for the project access control, lists the available groups and users. With the columns *read, add, edit*, and *delete* you customize the preferences according to your needs and save them.

Also the menu *projects Administration* comparatively provides few preferences. Here you can make three preferences:

- the selection of the administrators
- the selection of of the project sales department
- the editing of categories

There is no need to go into details for the category function. It has been described sufficiently above. Also the two functions *administration* and *sales department* are easy to handle. With the two dialogues it is possible to edit the according administrators resp. sales department. Thereby it is also possible to create multiple administrators.

7. Bookmark management

Another highlight of eGroupWare is the bookmark or also favourites management. In this modul the users save their links. The outstanding advantage against the browser bookmark management: The link collection is always available, namely independent from the own location. And: It can be easily provided to other users.

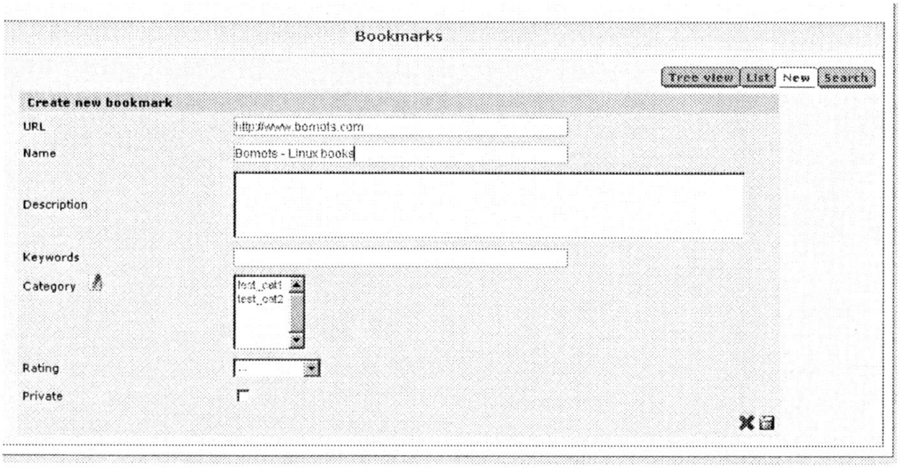

A new link arises.

Handling the bookmark management, like many other tasks under eGroupWare, is not problematical. The bookmark management is empty after a standard installation. This means for the user that he must insert his own links himself. To add a new link you click on the tab *New*. A form occurs with the following fields:

- **URL**: Here you fill in the link to the site.
- **Name**: The name or title of the page.
- **Description**: Here you type in a description of the link.
- **Keywords**: In this text field keywords can be deposited that imply the content of the link. The keywords are typed in with commas as delimiters.
- **Category**: Here the categorization of a link takes place.
- **Rating**: With this select menu the importance of a link can be provided with a rating on a scale from 1 for the lowest and 10 for the highest.
- **Private**: You activate this option in order that other users can not see this link.

In order to save the preferences you click on the disk icon in the right upper corner. After this eGroupWare presents an overview of the desired entries.

The bookmark management presents another three tabs:

- **Search**: If the link collection is very large, it can be comfortably searched by the search function. To do so, you click on the tab *Search* and enter the search item. Also the usage of logical operators is suported by the search.
- **Tree view**: With the tab *Tree view* you can open the individual categories and navigate through the collection similar to a file manager.
- **List**: The tab *List* displays a list of all links. But such a list is only useful for moderate collections. Nevertheless, with the according dialogue several functions are available, e.g. to edit links or also to send them by email. Also the deletion of links is possible here.

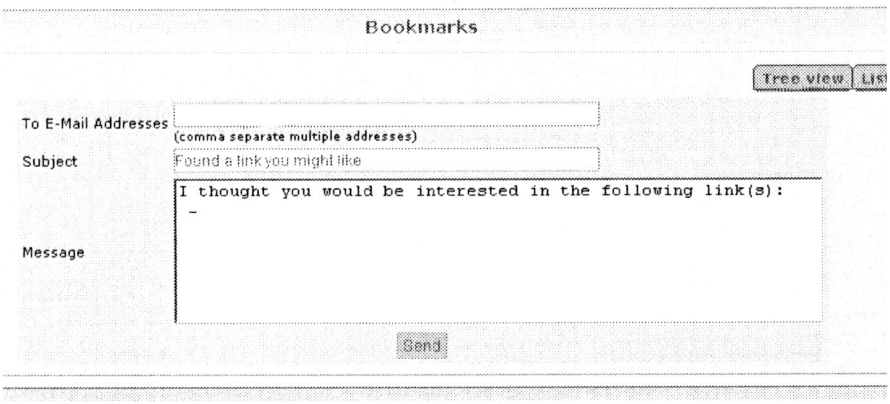

With the list resp. tree view links can even be sent per email.

But the bookmark module does not provide bookmark specific preferences. There is another limitation: The module doesn't provide the import of existing bokmarks.

8. Filemanager

With the file manager module a further useful tool is at the user's disposal. With his help users can execute typical file functions like uploading on the eGroupWare server, copying, moving etc. Not less interesting: The files can be authorized for other users. To do this one makes use of one of the access control lists.

According to the eGroupWare web site the *filemanager* module is still based on the developments for the phpGroupWare system. The original module was developed by Jason Wies and Jonathon Sim. Pim Snel has carried out the customizations necessary for eGroupWare.

The eGroupWare filemanager in rough state.

The most important file functions supported by the module are:

1. Uploading
2. Renaming
3. Copying
4. Moving
5. Creatingd drectories
6. Deleting
7. Creating and edting of text files
8. Synchronizing with the file system
9. Viewing file attributes
10. Navigating the directories

One part of the extended functions of the eGroupWare file manager is that one can also comment on files and also on lists. In addition, the file manager logs file changes. The advantage: Afterwards the changes be comprehended quite simply. Still there is a lack of the version controlling and restoration functions.

Until now, eGroupWare merely supports the release of files only via group access control lists. For the administrator this means that at first he must create a group in which all users who want to exchange files are listed. Independently, the access nevertheless can also be permitted by other groups and even single users.

Before one starts using the file manager, one should customize the file manager configuration in eGroupWare setup correspondingly (see section 2.19). There you follow the link *Check current configuration.* In the setup section, more clearly with the preferences *path information* and under *More settings*, there are two options important:

- *Complete path for user and group files*
- *Where to save and read the file informations*

At first you create a directory on the server into which the webserver can write. Then you enter these details as *Complete path for user and groups files* into the according input field. Thereby you use the absolute path. These preferences are important so that the filing can be used at all. If the settings are incorrect, the file manager gives out a corresponding error message. As a rule, you use under *More settings* SQL for the storage of file information (file type, file size, last modification etc.) and as a storage place the entry *Filesystem*. After you have typed in the suitable details, you save the configuration. Thus the file manager is ready for use.

8.1 Filemanager in practise

The filemanager is rather easy to handle. It presents two tool bars, the file and directory view and a status view. With the upper tool bar the following preferences are available:

- Up
- Back to home
- Reload
- Path view
- Quick jump
- Upload

The according functions are self-explanatory and therefore do not need further description. More interesting are the functions of the lower tool bar. With the two icons on the right you create new directories and add files to the filing. In both cases you enter a description in the input field on the left of the two icons and click on the desired icon.

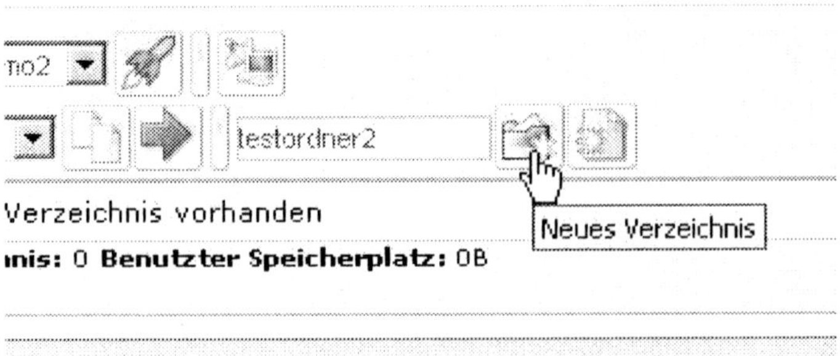

A new directory comes up in the filemanager.

To move files into the filing you click on the upload icon (disk antenna with monitor). In the appropriate dialogue you choose the file (or files) with *Browse* and then click on *Upload file*. The uploaded files will then be listed in the view.

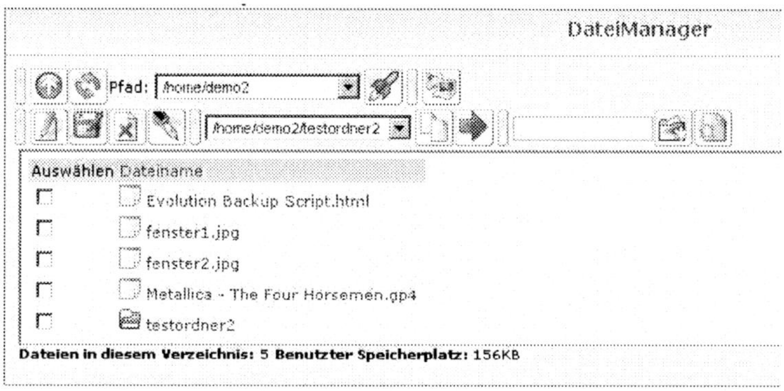

The filing gets full by and by.

With the filing you can delete objects by marking them, create and edit comments and perform all the file actions described above.

A real highlight of the filemanager is the file shares. The attentive reader might wonder where to find the according functions. You will not find the configuration of shares in the module *Filemanager*, but in the administrator area. In order to use this feature, you first of all need the appropriate rights. Only then you can assign shares.

And that's the way you proceed: First you create a group which contains all users who want to access the shared directories. It is important that the filemanager is selected in the list of the applications available. You then store the preferences in the document on which you also have activated the file manager for the group. A form with which the ACL rights are defined opens automatically. You should only assign rights the group here, but not to individual users. After this step you find a list under */home* with the group name used before. All members of the groups have access to the filing now.

8.2 Filemanager preferences

The filemanager also disposes of its own preferences, which are available with the filemanager menu. Here you can customize the filemanager according to the individual needs. As known from the other module preferences, administrators can also select defaults and force settings.

The form for the filemanager preferences allows the control of two areas: *Display attributes* and *Other settings*. The *Display attributes* settings are almost self-explanatory. Here you activate resp. deactivate the display of the following attributes:

- File name
- MIME Typ
- Size
- Created
- Modified
- Owner
- Created by
- Modified by
- Application
- Comment
- Version

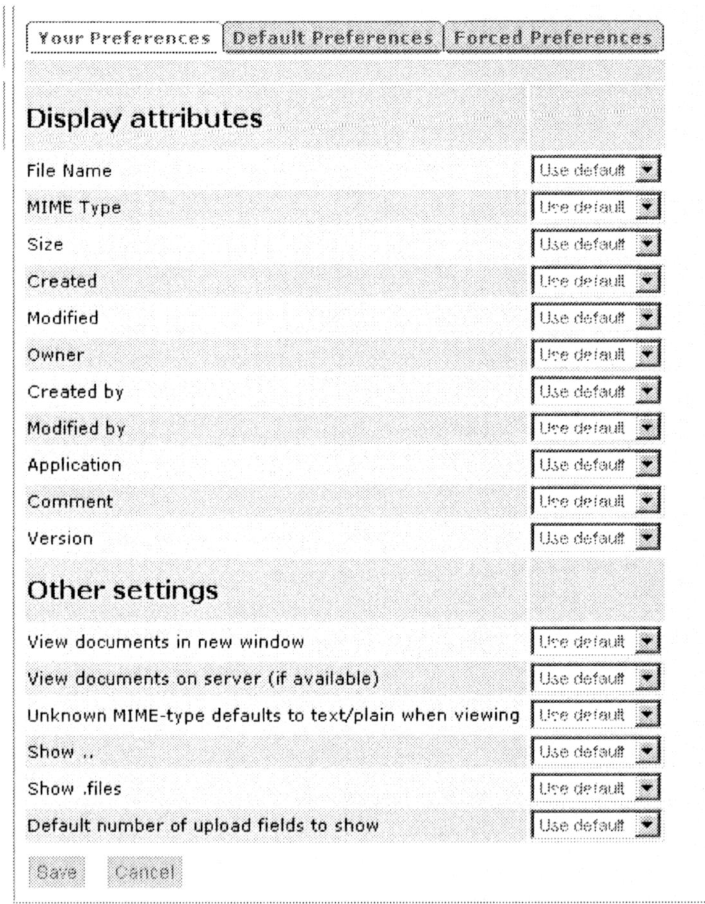

The filemanager preferences.

The functions of the area *Other settings* are summarized in the following chart:

Function	Descripton
View documents in new window	With the filemanager files are not only managed but can also be opened. Here you determine whether the documents should be opened in a new browser window or not. By default this is not applicable.
View documents on server (if available)	With this switch you determine whether the document should be shown on the server or not.
Unknown MIME-type defaults to text/plain when viewing	If you try to open a filetype unknown to eGroupWare, you can determine here whether the file should be opened as a text document.
Show ..	If you activate this setting, then in each directory the file... will be shown. This function is also deactivated by default.
Show .files	With this option you determine whether files that start with a dot should be listed or not.
Default number of upload fields to show	This option defines the number of fields when uploading files to the server. You can choose between the default 1, 5, 10, 20 and 30. With bigger values- the desired amount of lines can be found on the upload form (see the following illustration).

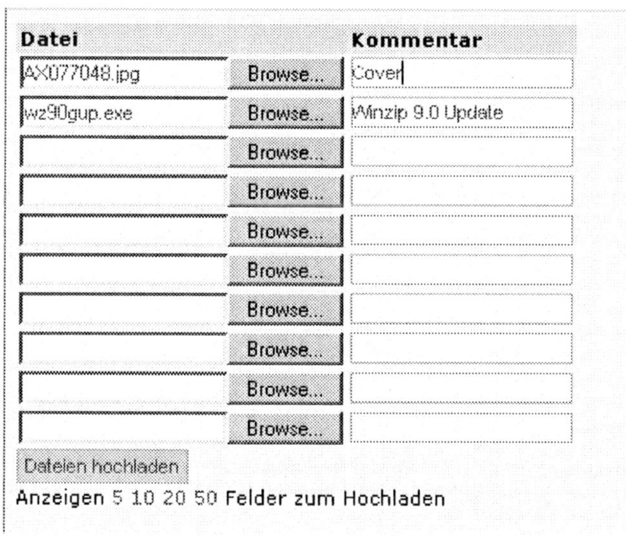

The form *Upload* now disposes of 10 fields.

9. Content management with SiteMgr

eGroupWare has a content management system of its own with the module *SiteMgr* with which web sites can be created. The ulterior motive: One doesn't only simply create a web site from the contents which the individual users produce but one goes back to already available components of the different eGroupWare applications.

Under eGroupWare these components are also called module – but they should not be confused with the eGroupWare modules. These components (blocks, modules or what ever they may be named) are constructed very flexible. They can fulfill site spanned, category or page specific tasks.

The SiteMgr module allows creating multiple sites that can be integrated into the eGroupWare environments. Besides, the module supports handling different versions of a content element. Your e.g. can create public open productivity elements and at the same time work on newer versions.

9.1 Basics

SiteMgr provides some more interesting functions. E.g. the content manager supports CSS, dXML import and export, the development of multilingual sites and templates. The SiteMgr module supports right now advanced Amazon and Google elements. There are more interesting features in development resp. planned, e.g.

- A powerful versioning, which allows the view at certain points in time.
- XML import and export of whole sites, categories and pages.
- Other modules as known from Mambo.
- Search function.

The content management system SiteMgr is, as typical for such environments, a template based system. The templates are by default stored in the directory */sitemgr/sitemgr-site/templates*. SiteMgr supports two template formats:

- The own, native format
- Mambo server templates (*www.mamboserver.com*)

The administrator can create his own templates or download a suitable template from the Mamboserver site and customize it according to his needs. At the Mamboserver site by the way you find hundreds of templates. There you also find tutorials how to create Mambo templates.

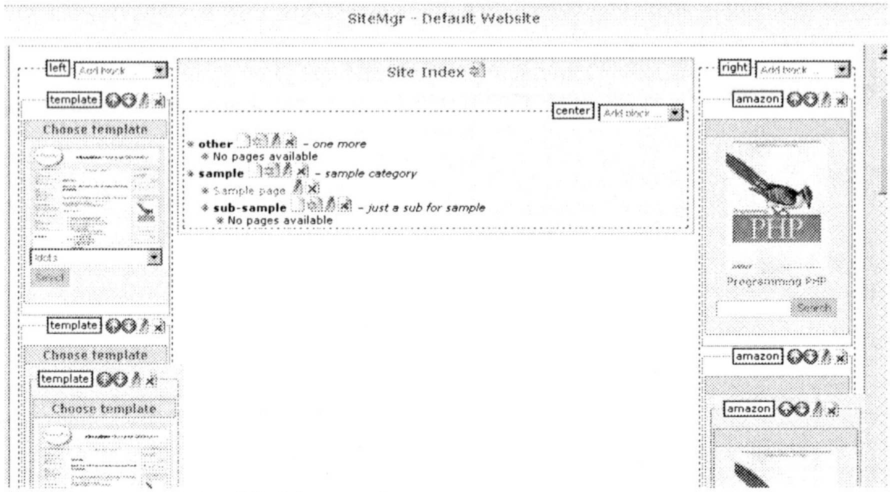

A first glance at the SiteMgr module.

We apply ourselves to the native siteMgr template format. The file *main.tpl* defines the site spanned template. With further files the individual areas are determined. Templates contain the following variables:

1. **contentarea: areaname**: It defines how the contents should be placed. Thereby the names and numbering of the content areas are almost arbitrary.
2. **modulename(?arguments)**: With this variable you define the module calls. The arguments have the syntax *HTTP GET (?key1=value1&key2=value2)*. An example: *lang_block* e.g. creates a multilingual select menu.
3. **?(phpgw|sitemgr:)link**: With this variable you create links to other pages of the website or to eGroupWare applications.
4. **variable**: With this variable you can ask for meta information of pages, e.g. *title* for the page title, *subtitle* for the subtitle, *sitename* for the site name, *sitedescription* for the description and *user* for the user name.
5. **lang_translatable_string**: Here you can internationalize your templates.

Here an example for the default template:

```
<!DOCTYPE html PUBLIC "-//W3C//DTD XHTML 1.1//EN"
"http://www.w3.org/TR/xhtml11/DTD/xhtml11.dtd">
<!-- $Id: main.tpl,v 1.5 2004/02/22 01:46:27 ralfbecker Exp
$ -->
<html xml:lang="en" xmlns="http://www.w3.org/1999/xhtml">
<head>
        <title>{sitename}: {title}</title>
        <meta http-equiv="content-type" content="text/html;
charset={charset}" />
        <meta http-equiv="expires" content="0" />
        <meta name="RESOURCE-TYPE" content="DOCUMENT" />
        <meta name="DISTRIBUTION" content="GLOBAL" />
        <meta name="AUTHOR" content="{sitename}" />
```

```
       <meta name="COPYRIGHT" content="Copyright (c) {year}
by {sitename}" />
       <meta name="DESCRIPTION" content="{slogan}" />
       <meta name="ROBOTS" content="INDEX, FOLLOW" />
       <meta name="REVISIT-AFTER" content="1 DAYS" />
       <meta name="RATING" content="GENERAL" />
       <meta name="GENERATOR" content="eGroupWare Web Site
Manager" />
       <meta name="keywords" content="eGroupWare" />
       <meta name="language" content="{lang}" />
       <link rel="icon"
href="templates/idots/images/favicon.ico" type="image/x-ico"
/>
       <link rel="shortcut icon"
href="templates/idots/images/favicon.ico" />
       {editmode_styles}
       <link href="templates/idots/style/style.css"
type="text/css" rel="StyleSheet" />
       <!-- This solves the Internet Explorer PNG-
transparency bug, but only for IE 5.5 and higher -->
       <!--[if gte IE 5.5000]>
       <script src="templates/idots/js/pngfix.js"
type=text/javascript>
              </script>
              <![endif]-->
       </head>

<body bgcolor="#ffffff" text="#000000" link="#363636"
vlink="#363636" alink="#d5ae83">
<div id="divLogo">
       <a href="index.php"><img
src="templates/idots/images/logo.png" border="0" ti-
tle="{site_name}" /></a>
</div>
<div id="divMain">
       <div id="divAppIconBar">
       <table width="100%" border="0" cellspacing="0" cell-
padding="0">
              <tr>
                     <td width="180" valign="top"
align="left"><img src="templates/idots/images/grey-
pixel.png" width="1" height="68" /></td>
                     <td>
                            <table width="100%" border="0"
cellspacing="0" cellpadding="0">
                                   <tr>
                                          <td width="100%"
height="68" align="center">
{contentarea:header}
                                          </td>
                                   </tr>
                                   <tr>
                                          <td
width="100%"> </td>
                                   </tr>
```

```
                        </table>
                </td>
                <td width="1" valign="top"
align="right"><img src="templates/idots/images/grey-
pixel.png" width="1" height="68" /></td>
            </tr>
        </table>
</div>

<div id="divSubContainer">
        <table width="100%" cellspacing="0" cellpadding="0">
            <tr>
                <td id="tdSideboxLeft">
{contentarea:left}
                </td>
                <td id="tdAppbox">
                        <div id="divAppboxHeader">{title}
{editicons}</div>
                        <div id="divAppbox">
                                <h3>{subtitle}</h3>
{contentarea:center}
                        </div>
                </td>
                <td id="tdSideboxRight">
{contentarea:right}
                </td>
            </tr>
        </table>
</div>
</div>
<div id="divFooter">
{contentarea:footer}
</div>

</body>
</html>
```

If you take a look into the directory where the templates are stored you will also find a XML file which describes the essential properties of a template. An example for *templateDetails.xml*:

```
<mosinstall type="template">
   <name>idots</name>
   <creationDate>2003/4</creationDate>
   <author>Ralf Becker</author>

 <copyright>
This template is relased under GPL as part of eGroupWare's
SiteMgr.
</copyright>
<authorEmail>RalfBecker@outdoor-training.de</authorEmail>
<authorUrl>www.eGroupWare.org</authorUrl>
<version>1.0</version>
```

```
 <description>
SiteMgr's idots template is based on Pim Snels phantastic
eGroupWare template-set.
 </description>
</mosinstall>
```

With the introduction of so called content elements as e.g. administration, calendar, google, login etc. the development of a site is simplified enormlously. The development of dynamic web site content is possible. With little effort these elements can be customized to the individual needs. To do so, you edit their properties. The easiest way to select such a component is the template. This of course assumes that they are suitable to do so.

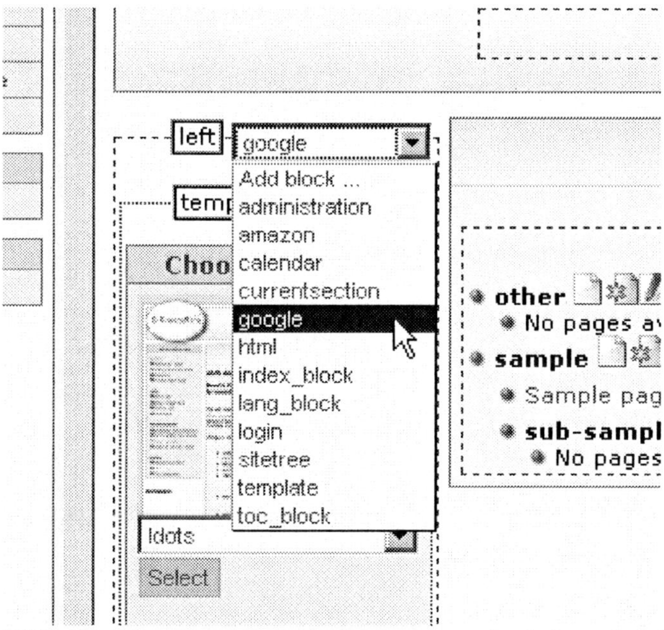

With SiteMgr new content elements can be integrated into a page with no problems.

The SiteMgr module handles the content elements (blocks) in versions. This means in practise: You can use multiple versions of a block, but only one of them is displayed in the website. The advantage: You can calmly test the different blocks and release them only if they achieve the desired effect. SiteMgr knows five status:

Status	Description
Draft	The draft does not appear on the website. As a matter of principle multiple drafts can be created and to a later point of time the best can be integrated into a website.
Prepublished	This type appears on the website, if it is viewed in

	preview mode. Such an element is registered for being published. It only lacks the allowance of the administrator for publishing it.
Published	An element with this status is already visible on the website and also in the preview mode.
Preunpublished	An element is set into this state if you want to delete or replace it.
Archived	Archived elements are no longer visible on the website. But they can be reactivated with the archive function.

9.2 Editing contents

The editing of pages and their contents is very easy – provided that you have the appropriate rights. The easiest is to first make some experiences with the demo website. The following illustration shows a typical content element with the according editing functions.

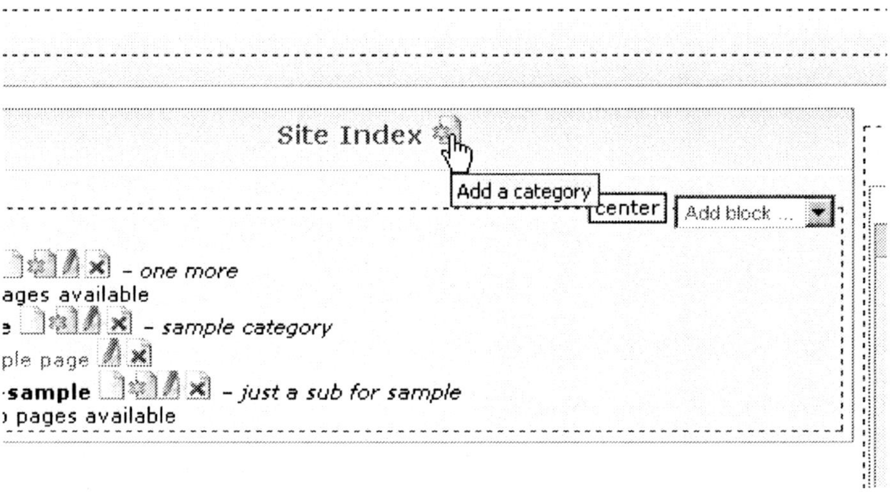

A typical content element in the edit mode.

For the most content elements the following properties are available:

- Add new page to the category
- Add category
- Edit category resp. block
- Delete category resp. block

Categories must be understood as a new text block within a content element (block). To create a new category at the desired position, you click on the according icon. A new window opens, in which you determine the preferences. Where new categories can be created is determined by the template.

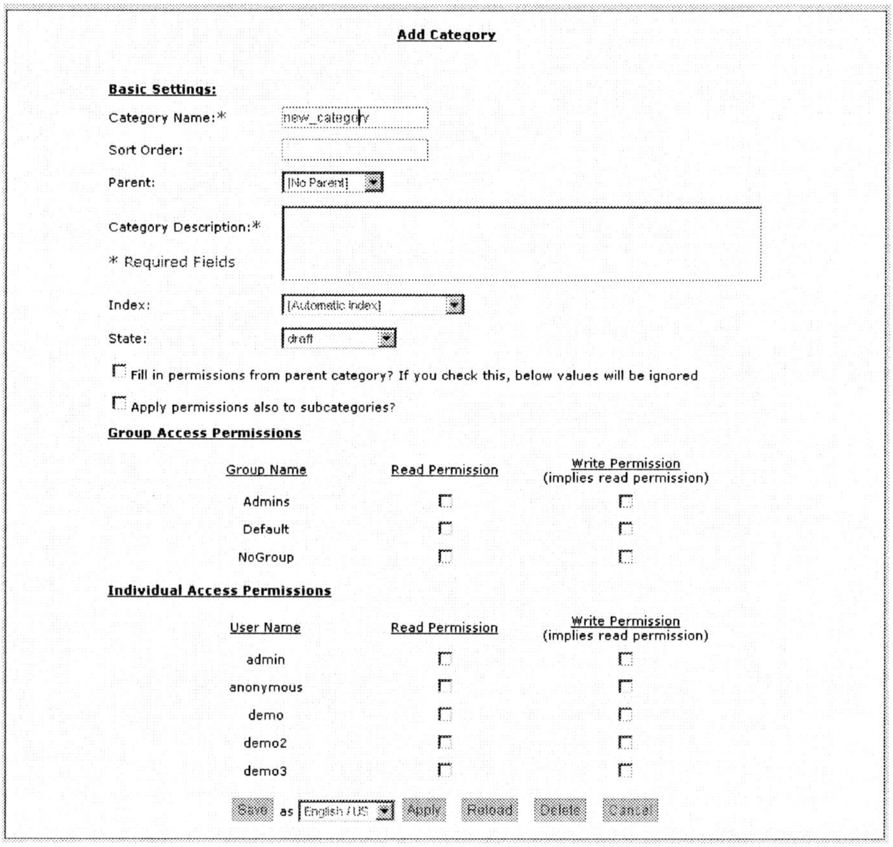

The dialogue for creating a new category.

With the form *Add form* you first determine the name and the sort order. Next follows a text field for the category description. Then you determine whether a table of contents should be generated automatically or not and which status the category takes temporarily (draft, prepublished etc.). Next follows the individual and user access rights. After a click on *Save* you get back to the edit view.

Mostly it follows the adding of a new page. This is easy, too. To do this, you click on the new page icon and in the according dialogue determine the age properties (see the following illustration).

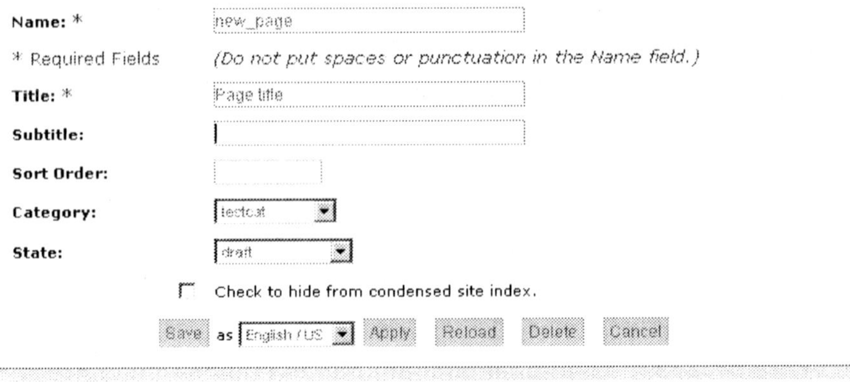

A new page is added to a block.

For the creation of content the editing of blocks is very important. Content blocks are indicated by a red dotted line. Besides the block name and a select menu for adding new blocks is displayed – as far as both functions are provided this way for the according elements in the template. As you can see in the following illustration, the block *index_block* is integrated into the block *left*.

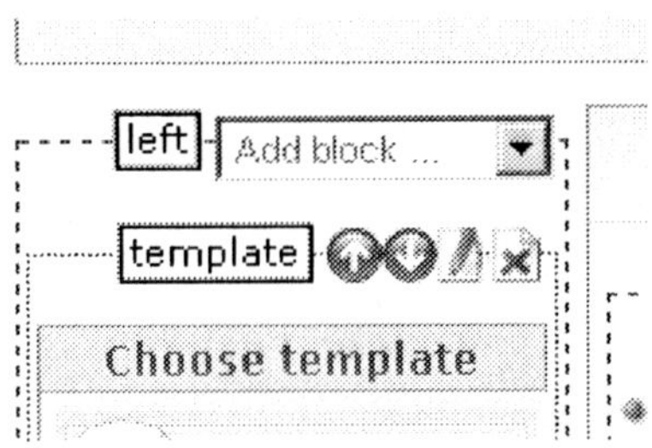

Content blocks and their edit functions.

If there are multiple blocks arranged one after another in a frame, as applicable for the above ilustration, they can be moved up or down by the green arrows. Besides editing and deleting is provided.

But how does one fill the created pages and categories with life? This is very easy, too. To do so, you help yourself using the block *HTML* that is available with the select menue *Add block*. In the select menu you just choose the entry *html*, and the HTML editor opens.

The editor provides all those functions you know from simple HTML editors. With the input field you compose your text and assign the desired formattings. Also inserting of web links, tables and graphics is possible in the editor.

After you have created the new HTML element and also provided it a title, *seen by* property and sort order, you click on *Save*. The new module will then be inserted at the desired position. At the upper frame border the module type *HTML* will be shown. The headline of the SiteMgr demo site, by the way, is a HTML element, too.

At the demo site the blocks available with the selection *Add blocks* are limited. These preferences can be edited by the so called modul manager. It is available with the link *Manage Site-wide module properties* of the website menue. The modul manager differentiates between the master list and the allowed modules for the different content areas. You can control exactly which modules should be site spanned and which ones should be allowed for certain areas. The selection is unproblematic: You mark an entry and then click on *Select allows modules*, so that the module is added from the list on the left to the list on the right.

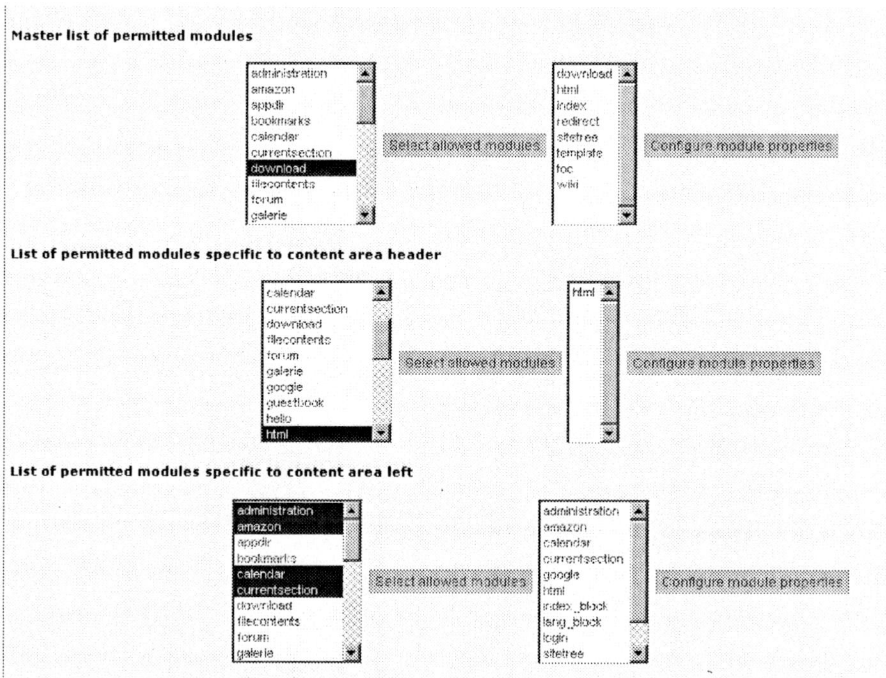

The module manager at work.

SiteMgr by default is delivered with the following modules.

- **Administration**: This module only creates a link to the administration interface of SiteMgr.
- **Amazon**: Shows an advertising for books of the Amazon website.
- **Appdir**: Demonstrates how to create an information directory.
- **Bookmark**: Can show the bookmarks of the eGroupWare application.
- **Calendar**: Shows the calendar entries of the eGroupWare calendar.
- **Currentsection**: Creates an index of the files in the current section.
- **Download**: Can create links to files that are managed by the eGroup-Ware file manager.
- **Filecontents**: Allows binding of content to a file.
- **Forum**: Shows discussion forums of a eGroupWare forum.

- **Gallery**: Creates an image gallery.
- **Google**: Shows a search form for the Google website.
- **Hello**: Shows a simple Hello world module.
- **Html**: The most important module for creating content indeed.
- **index_block**: Creates an index of the whole website.
- **lang_block**: Shows a select menu for the language translation.
- **Login**: Shows a typical login dialogue.
- **News**: Binds the news of the eGroupWare application of the same name.
- **Redirect**: Creates a redirect page to another URL.
- **Sitetree**: Creates a site tree.
- **toc_block**: Creates a table of contents.
- **Xml**: Demonstration that shows how to publish XML based contents.

9.3 Creating your own website

If one has become a little familiar with the content creating functions, the aim to build a website from the scratch arises soon. The SiteMgr-Modul is prepared for this purpose, too. To do this, you just click on the link *Configure Websites* in the menu *Other websites* (below the main menu). The according dialog presents a list of the already created sites. If you want to create a new site, you click on *Add*. With the form *Add Website* you determine the following preferences:

- **Site Name**: Here you deposit the website name that is used internally, indeed.
- **Filesystem path to sitemgr-site directory**: In this input field you enter the absolute path to the directory, e.g. */var/www/html/Your_Company/my_first_sitemgr_site/.*
- **URL to sitemgr-site**: In this input field you enter the absolute URL of the site. The indication must end with a slash, e.g. *http://my_domain/my_site/.*
- **Anonymous user's username**: With this administration menu you create a user that may use the public part of the site. Recommended username: *anonymous.*
- **Anonymous user's password**: Here you determine the password of the anonymous user.
- **Site administrators**: Finally you select the persons and groups from the select menu that are allowed to configure this website.

After a click on *Save* the preferences are accepted. In the upper area of the form the configuration may now take place with Configure *Website*. Here you determine the website name, descriptions, title, ID, meta information and languages used. Besides the design selection takes places here. After a click on *Save* the new site will be shown in the menu *Other Websites* and can be edited via the site name.

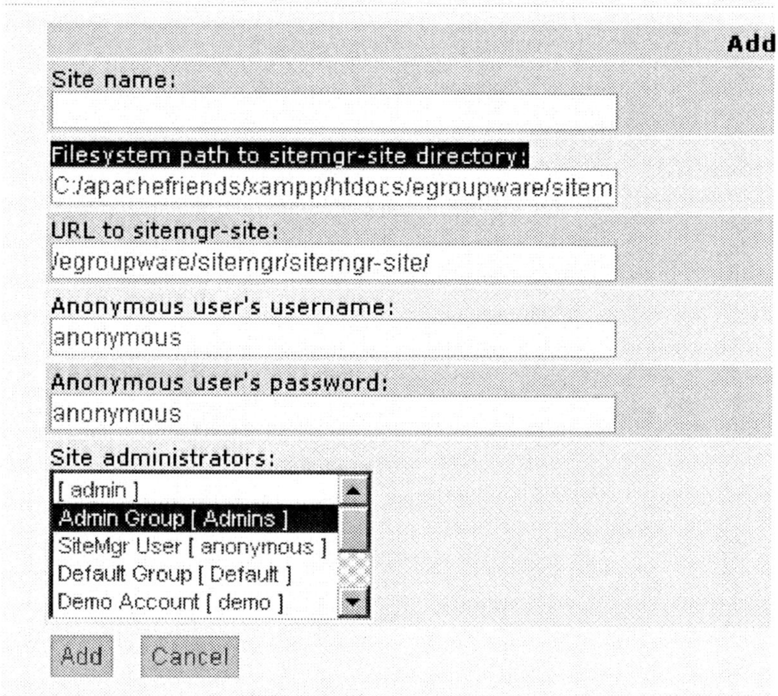

The configuration of a new website.

10. Creating eTemplates

Another highlight of eGroupWare is the module *eTemplate.* It is not quite for the use by „normal“ users but rather for the administrator and developer. With this tool you can create your own application for the eGroupWare system. What sounds complicated at the first glance need not be that complicated in practise, because the eTemplate module disposes of its own editor, with which many tasks can be simplified.

Therefore we follow the example of Ralf Becker of the eGroupWare team and create a media database for eGroupWare. This media database should contain the following fields: *name*, *author*, *description*, *type* (book, cd, video). Besides editing of the individual functions a search function should be integrated. To implement these requests, you besides the eTemplate editor grasp another two eTemplate tools: *DB-Tools* and *class.so_sql.inc.php.*

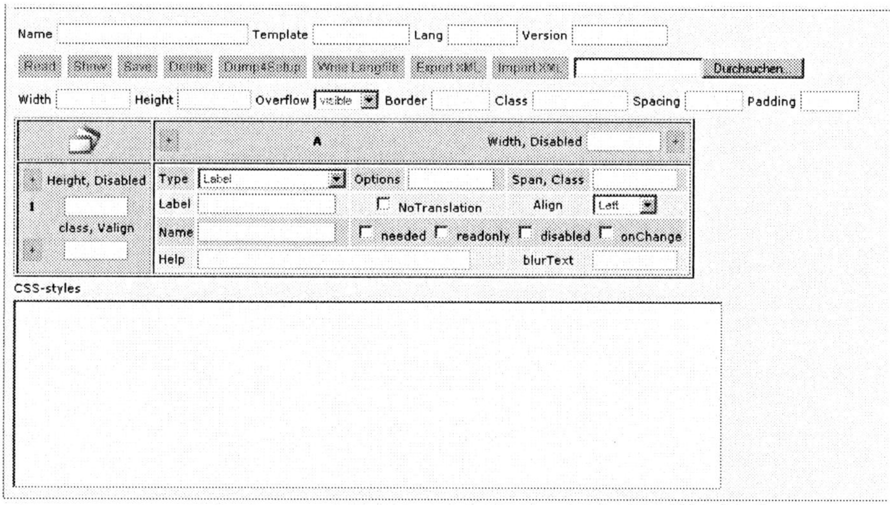

A first glance at the eTemplate module.

For the first step the above form is a worthful help. In the first step you assign a description to the application with the field *Name*, e.g. *media*. Besides the following directory tree must be created in the eGroupWare directory:

```
media_database                # application-ID
      setup                   # required setup files
      inc                     # class files
      templates               # templates
            default
               images         # images, icons
```

In the second step you create the file *media/setup/setup.inc.php*. In this file the information required for the setup is deposited:

```
<?php
	$setup_info['media']['name']      = 'media';
	$setup_info['media']['title']     = 'Media';
	$setup_info['media']['version']   = '0.9.15.001';
	$setup_info['media']['app_order'] = 100;
	// at the end
	$setup_info['media']['tables']                      =    ar-
ray('phpgw_media');
	$setup_info['media']['enable']    = 1;

	/* Dependencies for this app to work */
	$setup_info['media']['depends'][] = array(
		'appname' => 'phpgwapi',
		'versions'                  =>                 Ar-
ray('0.9.14','0.9.15','0.9.16')
	);
	$setup_info['et_media']['depends'][] = array( //  this
is only necessary as long the etemplate-class is not in the
api
		'appname' => 'etemplate',
		'versions'                  =>                 Ar-
ray('0.9.14','0.9.15','0.9.16')
	);
```

Next follows the third step with the setup of *db-table* by means of the DB-Tools. To do so, you click on the link *DB-Tools* in the eTemplate menu. Now the table has to be created. To do so, you perform the following steps:

1. First you choose from the select menu *application* the entry *media.*
2. Then you type in *phpgw_media* in the input field next the button *Add table* and hit Enter.

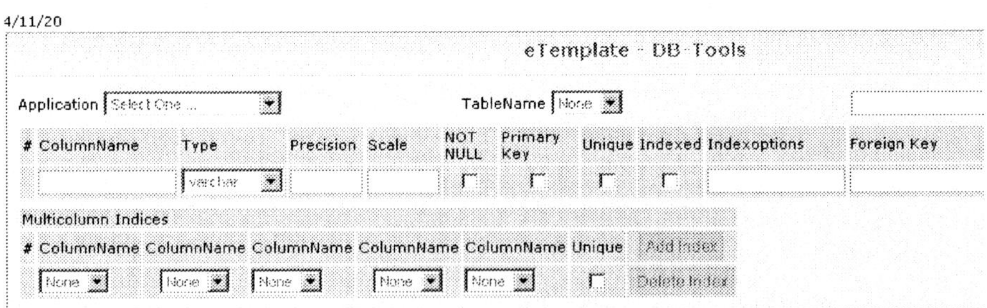

With the DB-Tools of eTemplate you create a new meda database.

3. Then you create according to the above illustration five columns. You should notice the *type* and the *precision*. After entering the first column name you click on *Add column*.
4. Next you click on *Write Tables*. The following dialogue asks, whether the changs should be saved. Affirm this question.
5. Now you log off, open the setup (advanced administration of the application) and activate the application there.

Next follow the step to create an eTemplate for the editing dialogue. To do so, you help yourself by the eTemplate editor. First you enter the desired description the field *Name*, e.g. *media.edit*. Then you create five field types, according to the following illustration. With the plus sign in the first line of the form you add more table columns. You implement five lines with the according types:

- Name (type description)
- Author (type description)
- Type (type description)
- Description (type description)
- Read (type button)

Besides you create a second column in which you fill in the following values:

- Name (type textfield, options 100,100)
- Author (type textfield, options 100,100)
- Type (type select box)
- Description (type textfield, options 100,100)
- Read (type button)

Explanations are filled in the form fields *Help*.

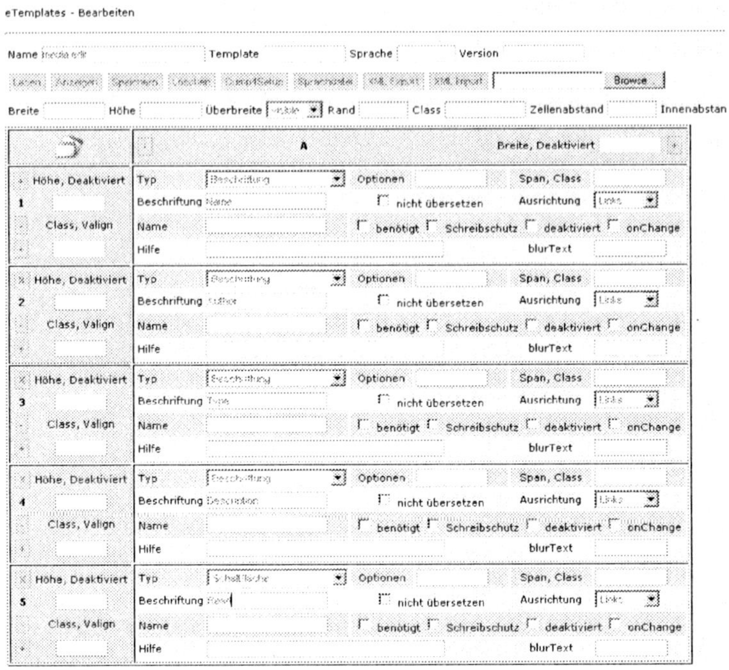

The form of the new media database assumes shape.

With the button *Save* you save the settings. The preview is activated with *Show (no save)*.

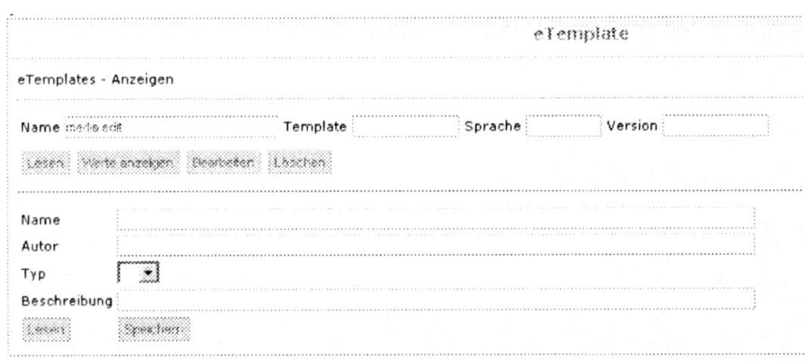

The preview of the new application.

Next follows the setup of the index page. It is only needed if a user clicks on the navbar icon. The index page should look like this:

```
<?php
        $GLOBALS['phpgw_info']['flags'] = array(
                'currentapp' => 'media',
                'noheader'   => True,
                'nonavbar'   => True
        );
        include('../header.inc.php');
```

```
        header('Location:                           '.$GLOBALS['phpgw']-
>link('/index.php','menuaction=media.media.edit'));
        $GLOBALS['phpgw_info']['flags']['nodisplay'] = True;
exit;
```

Now you create the file *class.media.inc.php*, which you save as */media/inc/class.media.inc.php*. The frst code bock serves for saving new entries:

```
<?php
/****************************************\
* eGroupWare - eTemplates - Tutoria Example - a simple Me-
diaDB *
* http://www.eGroupWare.org *
* Written by Ralf Becker <RalfBecker AT outdoor-training DOT
de> *
* -------------- *
*  This program is free software; you can redistribute it
and/or modify it *
*  under the terms of the GNU General Public License as pub-
lished by the   *
*  Free Software Foundation; either version 2 of the Li-
cense, or (at your  *
*  option) any later version. *
\**********************************/

/* $ Id: class.et_media.inc.php,v 1.2 2002/10/19 11:11:03
ralfbecker Exp $ */

include_once(PHPGW_INCLUDE_ROOT                              .
'/etemplate/inc/class.so_sql.inc.php');
$GLOBALS['phpgw_info']['flags']['included_classes']['so_sql'
] = True;
```

The following code bock loads the class *so_sql*:

```
class et_media extends so_sql
{
        var $types = array(
                '' => 'Select one ...',
                'cd' => 'Compact Disc',
                'dvd' => 'DVD',
                'book' => 'Book',
                'video' => 'Video Tape'
        );
```

There will follow several messages that inform the user what happens:

```
        function media()
        {
                $this->tmpl                    =              CreateOb-
ject('etemplate.etemplate','media.edit');
```

```
                $this->so_sql('media','phpgw_media');   //   sets
up our storage layer using the table 'phpgw_media'
                $this->empty_on_write = "''";            //   what
to write in the db, if a column is empty, the default is
NULL

                $this->public_functions += array(        //   this
function     can     be     called     external,     eg.     by
/index.php?menuaction=...
                    'edit' => True,
                    'writeLangFile' => True
                );
        }
```

The final code block describes the creator of the class. It undertakes the following three tasks:

1. It creates a template object and loads the media.show template.
2. It sets up a storage layer in order that *so_sql* can read, write, delete, and search the entries in the SQL dateabase.
3. Finally it extends the public_functions array.

The final code block of the file *class.media.inc.php*:

```
        function edit($content='',$msg = '')
        {
                if (is_array($content))    // we are called as
callback for the dialog / form
                {
                    if ($content['id'] > 0)          // if we
have an id --> read the entry
                    {
                        $this->read($content);
                    }
                    $this->data_merge($content);     // merge
content with our internal data-array ($this->data)

                    if (isset($content['save']))     //   save
the entry ($this->data)
                    {
                        $msg     .=     !$this->save()      ?
lang('Entry saved') : lang('Error: writeing !!!');
                    }
                    elseif (isset($content['read']))
                    {
                        unset($content['id']);
                    // not set by user, so dont use for seach
                        $found              =           $this-
>search($content,False,'name,author'); // searches by using
the no-empty fields

                        if (!$found)                 //
search returned empty
                        {
```

```
                                $msg    .=    lang('Nothing
matched search criteria !!!');
                          }
                          else
                          {
                                $this->init($found[0]);
      // set data-array with the content of the first match
                          }
                    }
              }

              // now we filling the content array for the
next call to etemplate.exec

              $content = $this->data + array(  // the content
to be merged in the template
                    'msg' => $msg
              );
              $sel_options = array(           // the options
for our type selectbox
                    'type' => $this->types
              );
              $no_button = array(       // button not to show
              );
              $preserv = array(         // this data is pre-
served over the exec-call (like a hidden input-field in
form)
                          'id' => $this->data['id']
              );
              $this->tmpl->exec(
                    'et_media.media.edit',    // setting this
function as callback for the dialog
                    $content,$sel_options,$no_button,$preserv
              );
      }
}
```

With these steps the basic functionality of the media database is realized. You now can save new entries and search the database. What lacks is e.g. the option to show multiple matches. How to reach this is described in the eTemplate tutorial. Developers will find additional information in the eTemplate Referenz.

11. Additional modules

eGroupWare is, as we have seen several times, a modular environment to a high degree. Each administrator can scope out of a pool of almost thirty components. You hardly can ask more flexibility. Besides the modules described above the following modules are available (in alphabetical order):

- Backup
- Comics
- Forum
- Headlines
- JiNN
- Knowledge Base
- News
- Notifywindow
- phpldapadmin
- Polls
- Registration
- Stock Quotes
- Translation Tools
- Trouble Ticket System
- Wiki

This final chapter gives an overview on the remainig modules. How to activate the modules for individual users or groups is described in chapter 2.

11.1 Stock Quotes

With the module *Stock Quotes* eGroupWare can retrieve selected quotations of shares from *finance.yahoo.com* and show them on the main screen.

11.2 Comics

The Comics function gives variety in the sometimes stressful everyday life at work. Here you can create your own entertainment program out of different internet sources. To do so, you first activate the Comics module and then open the menu *Preferences*.

There you first select one of the two formats for the presentation of the drawings. Besides, different display options can be defined. With the select menu at the bottom of the document area the actual selection of the comic takes place. With a click on *Done* you accept the changes. The comic is now integrated into the system.

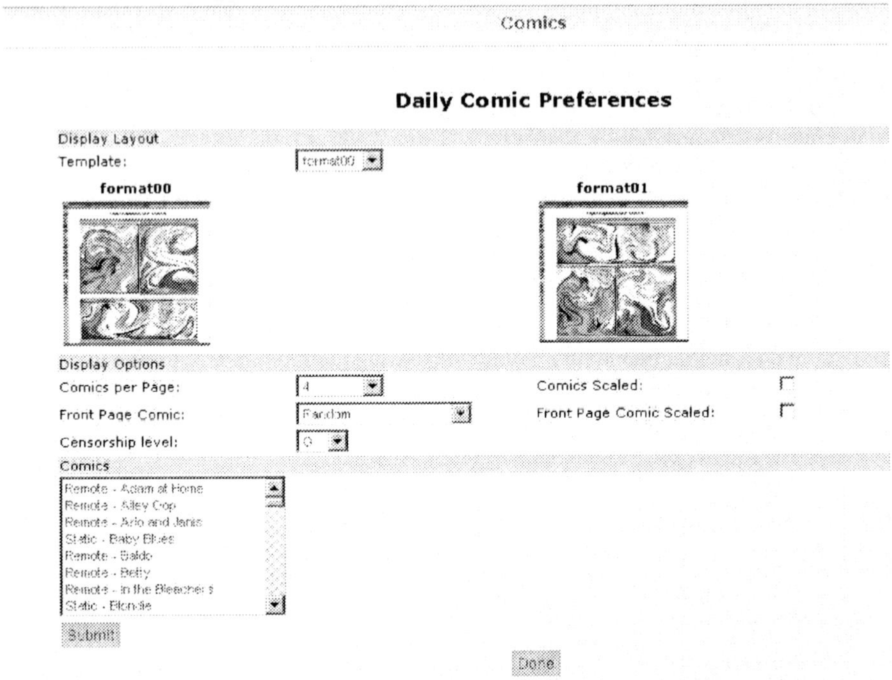

The Comic module – so that the fun with work doesn't drop out.

Also the Comics module has its own administration menu. It provides two functions:

- Global Options
- Global Comics

With the global options you particularly define the preferences for the censorship level, the image source and the maximum file size. A look into the preferences of the global comics shows the offers you can choose from. There are far more than 100 comic sources listed there.

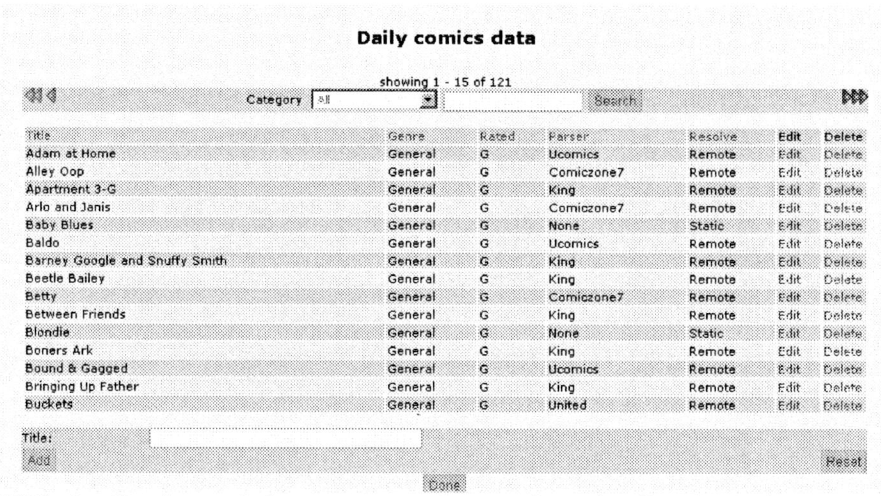

Daily comics data

showing 1 - 15 of 121

Category [All] Search

Title	Genre	Rated	Parser	Resolve	Edit	Delete
Adam at Home	General	G	Ucomics	Remote	Edit	Delete
Alley Oop	General	G	Comiczone7	Remote	Edit	Delete
Apartment 3-G	General	G	King	Remote	Edit	Delete
Arlo and Janis	General	G	Comiczone7	Remote	Edit	Delete
Baby Blues	General	G	None	Static	Edit	Delete
Baldo	General	G	Ucomics	Remote	Edit	Delete
Barney Google and Snuffy Smith	General	G	King	Remote	Edit	Delete
Beetle Bailey	General	G	King	Remote	Edit	Delete
Betty	General	G	Comiczone7	Remote	Edit	Delete
Between Friends	General	G	King	Remote	Edit	Delete
Blondie	General	G	None	Static	Edit	Delete
Boners Ark	General	G	King	Remote	Edit	Delete
Bound & Gagged	General	G	Ucomics	Remote	Edit	Delete
Bringing Up Father	General	G	King	Remote	Edit	Delete
Buckets	General	G	United	Remote	Edit	Delete

Title:

Add Reset

Done

With the Comics module you can use dozens of comic offers in the internet.

11.3 Backup

With the module *Backup* there is another useful tool available for the eGroupWare user. Here it is possible to save mails, appointments etc. with the appropriate means. The backup module is the optimum addition of traditional backup methods like system backup or mirror. If you access the module for the first time, eGroupWare shows the following error message:

```
The backup application is not configured for showing the archives in eGroupWare yet!
```

In order to use the backup, it must be set up via the admin module. To do so, you first open the preferences of the application. In the appropriate form you fill in the program paths for the packer to be used. Next is the path information for the files to backup.

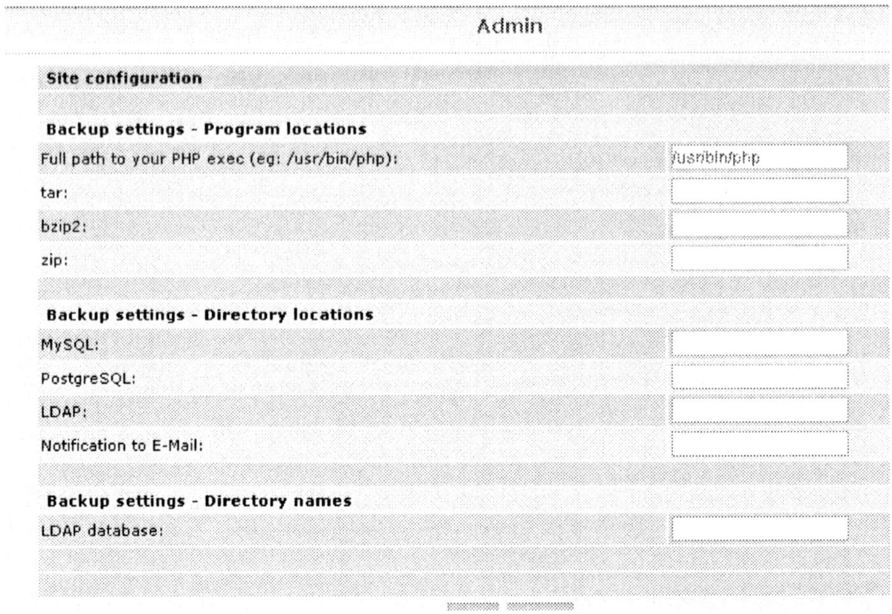

The configuration of the backup.

If you have set these preferences, then you follow the link *Backup Administration*. Here you determine whether data backups should be produced at all and, in case of yes, in which interval. You then select which data you want to save and which archive type you prefer. Next follow the preferences, on which local and/or remote computer should be backed up. The backup is ready for use now and the control can be carried out via the module *backup*.

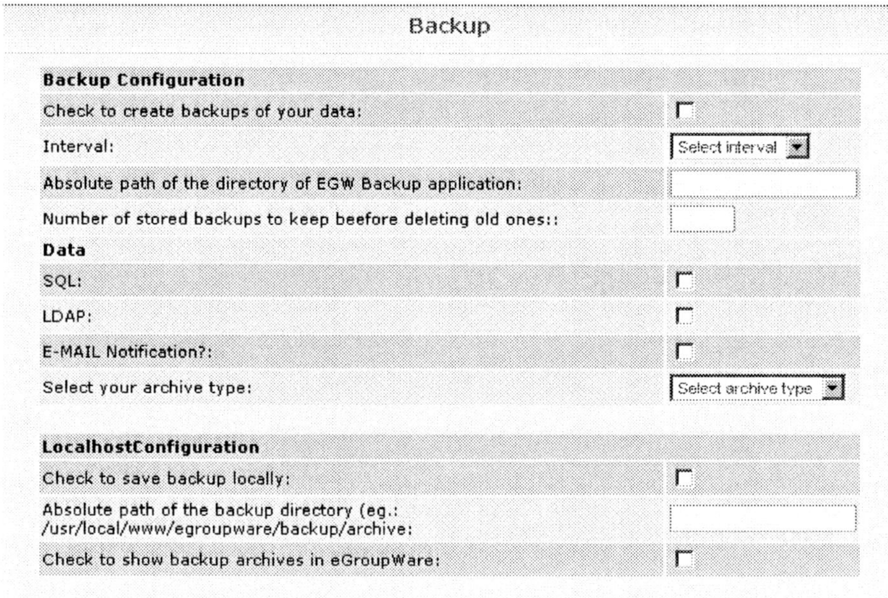

The data backup won't work without the correct configuration via the backup administration.

11.4 Forum

Behind the forum modul a typical online forum hides, in which users discuss a variety of topics. Important to the administrator resp. the one who wants to establish a forum of its own is the forum administration. With it you create new forum categories and new forums. Within a category you then can set up any desired forum. With the forum button of the tool bar you get to the forum view. It allows selecting themes as well as creating new articles.

11.5 JiNN

JiNN stands for Jinn Is Not Nuke. But it is also an Arab term for spirit or genie. This module is a content manager which serves the management of several sites, multiple databases and also users and groups. JiNN can be understood as a database managment system, with which many users can manage and use content elements. The access rights are all located on table level. Besides, each site owns one or even multiple administrators.

11.6 News

With the *news* module it is possible to publish news on the eGroupWare site. With the *News Admin* you create new articles including title, teaser and content. Besides you determine the category on the appropriate form.

11.7 Notifywindow

The module *Notifywindow* is available with the homepage of a eGroupWare installation. Here notifications on new mails, project belongings etc. are listed.

11.8 phpLDAPadmin

phpLDAPadmin is a web based LDAP browser and editor. With its help you can navigate through the LDAP tree, create, delete, edit, and copy entries. Also searching for entries and the import and export from resp. to LDIF is possible. The module can also use several LDAP servers.

11.9 Registration

The accout registration module provides the typical functions for the login of users in an eGroupWare environment. Also this module is already preconfigured, ready to use, and must only be configurated via the registration administration.

With the admin form for the configuration of the registration, you first activate it, and then determine, whether there should be an appropriate link added on the login page with which users can register. Besides you determine the preferences for the email notifcation and the terms of use.

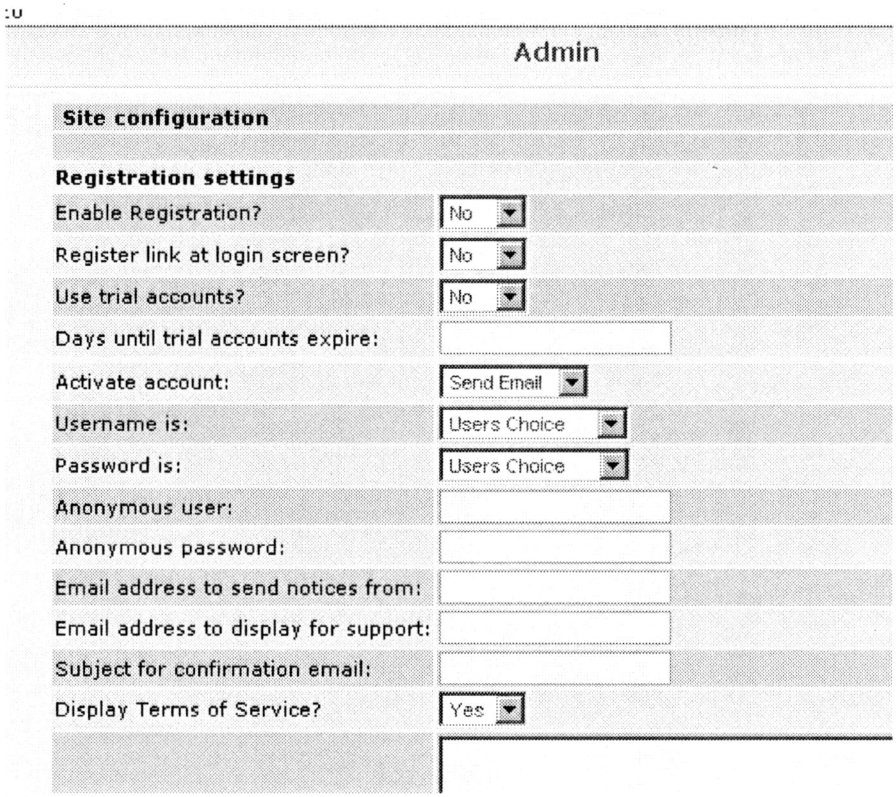

Die configuration of the registration.

With the login dialog and the link added there resp. with the register icon you get to the actual registration form. Here you determine the desired user name and select the language. With the link *Submit* you get to the form for *User Account Registration*. Here you fill in the following information:

- password
- re-enter password
- birthday
- email
- first name
- last name
- address
- city
- state
- ZIP/postal
- country

The statements on the telephone number and the gender are optional. Besides, the terms of use must be accepted. The system states the successful registration and indicates that an affirmation mail will be sent.

11.10 Headlines

The module *Headlines* retrieves, similar to the module *Comics*, news from the internet. These are news services that are made available by different providers. The headlines module of eGroupWare thereby uses the RDF based services. RDF (Resource Description Framework) is a specification for the representation of meta data. This is a XML based language which is also used for the provision of news.

With the headlines preferences about a dozen news services are available. To use one or more, you mark it and click on *Save*. They will then be listed in the headlines view. With the link *Headline Site Management* you can not only edit existing ones but also add new sources.

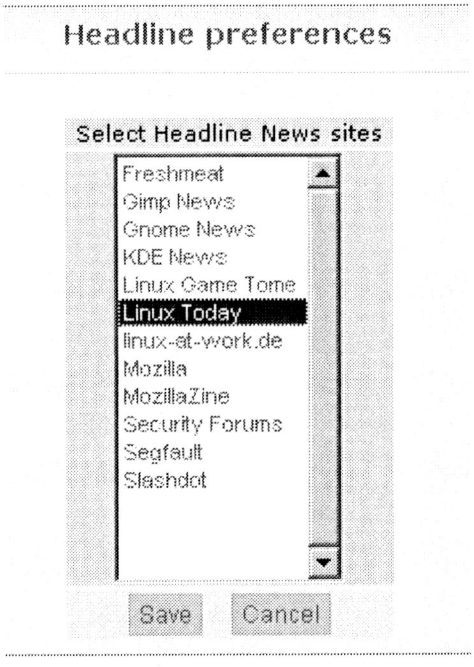

The selection of the headlines.

11.11 Trouble Ticket System

The *trouble ticket system* is a support module which was conceived especially for the processing of support enquiries. It supports delegating and pursuing customer demands. It is a very flexible system which can be adapted to the most different requirements. An important aspect is the persuing of an enquiry. Therefore inquiries are to be treated as a ticket.

To produce a new ticket, you click in the ticket system on *New Ticket* and feed the according form with the corresponding information. Thereby it will be assigned to an employee or a group, the priority fixed, the exit status and invoice preferences determined as well as a subject allocated and a description attached. After storing the ticket lands in the so-called ticket list.

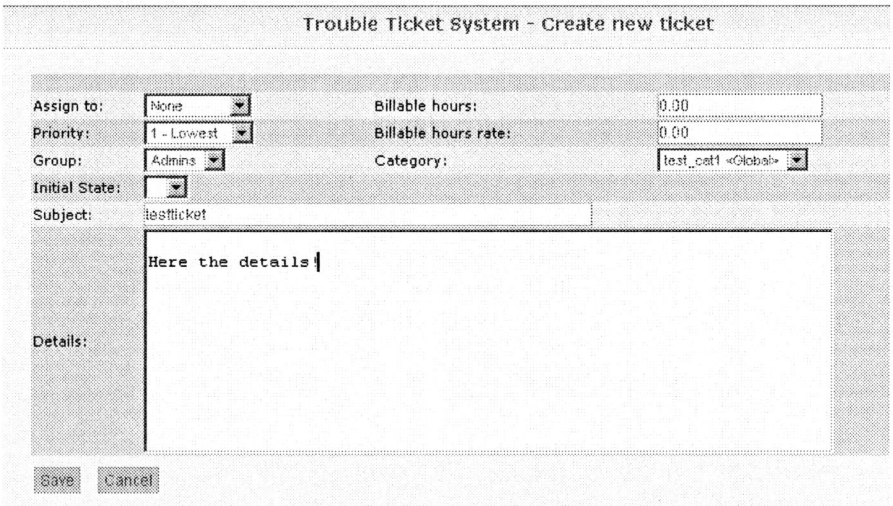

A new ticket arises.

With the job details the real work is carried out. Besides general information you find different information, for example

- Detail information like the ticket opening date and notes.
- Information about the state of the inquiry, for example the assignments to a new editor.
- Notes of all changes.

Further preferences are available with the trouble ticket system administration., e.g. options for the mail notification and the status configuration.

11.12Polls

The importance of the *polls* module is obvious to everybody: With this module you can create typical polls as known from many websites. E.g. you can let the customers rate the content or ask for additional information. With the polls preferences you create new polls including the according questions and the possible answers.

11.13 Wiki

Wikis, also called WikiWikis and WikiWebs, are encyclopaedias available in the web. They are collections of pages that can not only read by the users but also edited online. The name is derived from the Hawaiian word for "quick". They are free projects that currently at a tearing speed gain content und therefore gain more importance. The Wiki integrated in eGroupWare is based on WikkiTikkiTavi (tavi.sourceforge.net).

11.14 Knowledge Base

The module *Knowledge Base* is comparable to Wiki, because also Wiki is nothing more than such a database. Both allow creating and managing of documents.

11.15 Translation Tools

The last module is the so called translation tools. As eGroupWare is a multilingual environment, you also need functions to customize the translations. With the translation tools you can customize the default for each description, message etc.

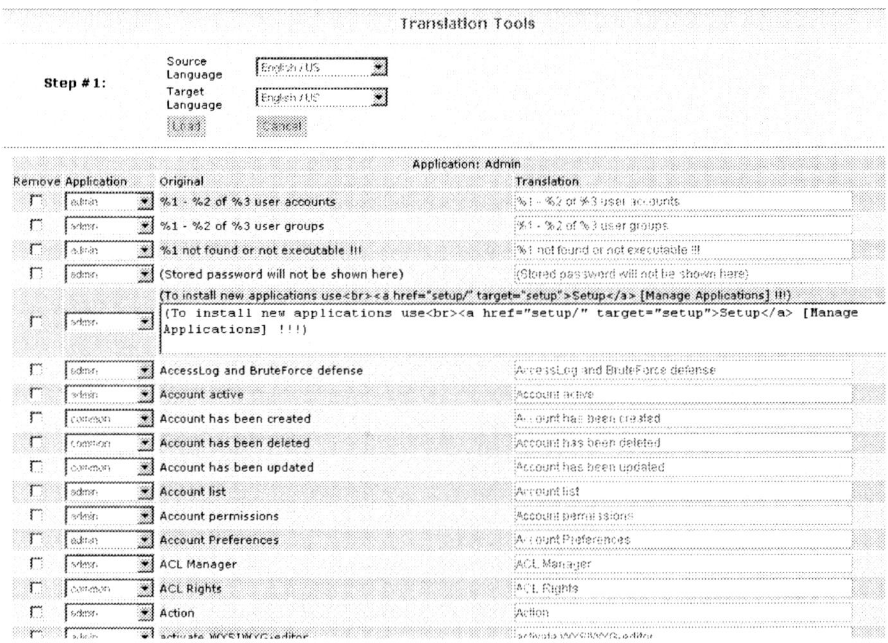

The translation tools of eGroupWare.

Appendix – further sources

It is quite natural for an introductory pocket book that there will be some questions left. To all those who want to learn more about eGroupWare, we recommend the following three web sites:

- **eGroupWare.org** (*www.egroupware.org*): The official eGroupWare homepage. Here you find almost everything you need: Recent messages, download links, different documents and several mailing lists.

- **eGroupWare Security Install & Security HowTo Ver. 0.4** (*www.egroupware.org/?category_id=27*): Detailed HowTo to secure installation and usage of eGroupWare, written by the chief developer himself.

- **Sourceforge.net** (*sourceforge.net/projects/egroupware/*): The eGroupWare project pages on Sourceforge. Here you find besides a general overview recent downloads and brandnew downloads and several discussion groups.

Index

Printed in the United Kingdom
by Lightning Source UK Ltd.
112448UKS00001B/178